Praise

M000304453

The Checklist Life reminds us that we aren't meant to do life alone. Tracy's reflections on her own life and the lives of other women is vulnerable, authentic, and relatable. The life lessons shared throughout the book are applicable to so many of us on so many levels. *The Checklist Life* will easily become the book you gift to your sister, aunt, best friend, the new mom at work, and your neighborhood gal pals. It's a perpetual reference guide you won't want to leave home without.

—*JESSICA DUDLEY*
Assessor, Jarvis Township

The Checklist Life is the perfect handbook for women who want to live a more authentic life. The book is the toolbox to get readers thinking, and the questions and action items at the end of each chapter are the ideal tools to fill that toolbox.

—*SHARI ALBRECHT*
Executive Director, JEDC Partners in Progress, Inc.

This is an amazing and easy read! Tracy's stories are sincere and relatable to any woman searching for her authentic self. *The Checklist Life* is the perfect roadmap for living your best life!

—*LAURA MATTSON*
Business Development Officer, First Community Credit Union

The Checklist Life is an invitation into Tracy's world, a world that mirrors my own in so many ways. The takeaway stories and ideas, the end-of-chapter questions, and the action plan suggestions allow readers to think about their own life—why we are here, who we choose to have in our life, and how being vulnerable is tough but, in the end, is what sets us free. So many women are sure to benefit from this book!

> —*DAWN MUSHILL*
> *CEO, Customer Service & Beyond*

If you are stressed, overwhelmed, and barely keeping up with all of life's demands, put this book on the top of your must-read list! Respected leadership coach Tracy Bianco inspires women to live their best life by sharing the wisdom she came by honestly, in a very human and compelling way. I recommend this book to my clients, and I wholeheartedly recommend it to anyone who's craving a more authentic, gratifying life journey!

> —*TRACY BARANAUSKAS*
> *Moving Forward Life Coaching*

The Checklist Life is the book I've always needed in my life. I grew up following a checklist life like the one Tracy describes. I completed all of my obligations and did what was expected but often found myself stressed, overwhelmed, and unsatisfied. This book shows you how to throw away your old expectations, breaking free from the life you thought you should want, so you can live the fulfilling life you deserve. Tracy's authenticity and humor captured my attention and made this an easy read.

> —*COURTNEY WRIGHT*
> *Financial Advisor, Benjamin F. Edwards & Co.*

The Checklist Life is a personal look at how we can change our lives from doing what's expected by others—and even by ourselves—to a life that offers fulfillment on another level.

Tracy's story—and the pain and uncertainty within it—will captivate you as you relate to her inner conflicts. *The Checklist Life* gives readers the opportunity to absorb and think and make decisions to pivot in a way that offers them freedom.

—DR. SUSAN HARRISON
Founder & CEO, Dr. Susan Harrison

Tracy's philosophy is that the things we do and how we feel about the world around us are deeply rooted in the stories we tell ourselves and the beliefs they create. With stories of her journey to find peace and balance in her own life, she offers a view that every woman can relate to, along with the revelation that we each have what it takes to rewrite our inner stories. Tracy offers compassionate and empathetic guidance on how to do just that, so we can lead the kind of life we want.

Not afraid to reveal her own vulnerabilities and struggles, Tracy writes with authenticity and grace. She's not preaching from a pulpit—she's down here learning and growing along with the rest of us.

—RITA DUCKWORTH
Owner, Rita Duckworth Writing & Editing

The Checklist

LIFE

The Checklist LIFE

BREAKING FREE FROM A LIFE OF OBLIGATIONS

Tracy Bianco

Stonebrook Publishing
Saint Louis, Missouri

STONEBROOK PUBLISHING

A STONEBROOK PUBLISHING BOOK
©2020 Tracy Bianco

This book was guided in development and
edited by Nancy L. Erickson, The Book Professor®
TheBookProfessor.com

The stories in this book are true, but the names have been changed
to protect the privacy of those involved.

Library of Congress Control Number: 2020908100
ISBN: 978-1-7347340-0-3

www.stonebrookpublishing.net

PRINTED IN THE UNITED STATES OF AMERICA

10 9 8 7 6 5 4 3 2 1

Dedication

*For the extraordinary women who juggle so much
every day and ask themselves if they're doing it right.
You are remarkable. You are incredible.
You make the world a better place.
I offer you the lessons that took me far too long to learn
with the wish that they will help you live your very best life.*

Contents

ACKNOWLEDGMENTS   **xiii**

CHAPTER 1: Understand It to Change It   **1**

CHAPTER 2: Stop the Box Checking   **7**

CHAPTER 3: Lead with Pride   **12**

CHAPTER 4: Build the Belief   **19**

CHAPTER 5: Live in a New Neighborhood   **24**

CHAPTER 6: Mix in Some Self-Care   **29**

CHAPTER 7: Give Yourself Some Grace   **34**

CHAPTER 8: Paint Your Masterpiece   **39**

CHAPTER 9: Squash the Shame   **45**

CHAPTER 10: Create Your Tribe   **50**

CHAPTER 11: Venture into Vulnerability   **55**

CHAPTER 12: Learn from the Best   **60**

CHAPTER 13: Block the Boomerang Life   **66**

CHAPTER 14: Kick Comfort to the Curb   **71**

CHAPTER 15: Rise Up with Resilience   **76**

CHAPTER 16: Own the New You   **82**

CHAPTER 17: Forge Your New Path   **88**

CHAPTER 18: Find Some New Firsts   **93**

CHAPTER 19: Make the Proof Go Poof   **99**

CHAPTER 20: Take Responsibility   **104**

CHAPTER 21: Travel Your New Path   **110**

CHAPTER 22: Dive into Uncharted Territory   **115**

CHAPTER 23: Talk to Your Truth Tellers   **121**

CHAPTER 24: Unlock the Cuffs   **127**

CHAPTER 25: Ditch the Excuses   **133**

CHAPTER 26: Focus on Your Wins   **139**

CHAPTER 27: Teach Your Brain Some New Tricks   **144**

CHAPTER 28: Slow Down the Checklist Ride   **149**

CHAPTER 29: Flatten Your Fear   **154**

CHAPTER 30: Halt the Busy Train   **160**

CHAPTER 31: Kick It Into Gear with Self-Confidence   **165**

CHAPTER 32: Build Your Boundaries   **171**

CHAPTER 33: Push Forward with an Accountability Partner **176**

CHAPTER 34: Champion Your Most Desired Changes   **182**

CHAPTER 35: Make Life Your Own Magnificent Marathon   **187**

ABOUT THE AUTHOR   **191**

Acknowledgments

Many thanks to my husband, Jim, who has been by my side through it all. We've grown up together, and you support me like no other. You make me a better me, and I'm so blessed to do life with you.

CHAPTER 1

Understand it to Change it

*"Until you make the unconscious conscious,
it will direct your life and you will call it fate."*
— C. G. JUNG

I **awoke to a warm,** wet feeling. What was happening? It
took just a few seconds for me to realize I'd wet the bed.
Not such a strange occurrence for a three-year-old, but I
wasn't three. I was eighteen. And I was pregnant.

The day my college-freshman self wet the bed was also
my dad's fifty-fifth birthday, just three days after Christmas.
A rule follower from Day One, this time I hadn't followed
the rules, and I knew it was time to tell my parents about
my pregnancy. The restless night and the drenched sheets
were the result of thoughts that had been spinning in my
head over the past two weeks. The stress of my secret
finally got to me. How could I break this news to them?

I had made it through the Christmas holiday with my parents, siblings, and huge extended family. It was uncomfortable because, one month prior, I'd made the unpopular decision (according to my parents) to transfer from my current college—over two hours away—to a local university. This meant I'd stay home after the holiday break.

Things were about to get even more uncomfortable. I now needed to tell my parents that their daughter would be a very young mom in a few short months.

I didn't plan to ruin Dad's birthday. And I didn't plan to wet the bed, either. How could I get those drenched sheets from my second-floor bedroom to the basement laundry area when my June Cleaver-esque mother was busy throughout the house doing everything for everyone?

With my sheets wadded in a ball, I tiptoed down the steps and made a mad dash for the basement. And there was Mom.

"Why do you have your sheets, Tracy?" You see, it wasn't strip-the-bed day. That was on Tuesday each week.

"Ummm . . . I thought I'd throw them in the wash," I fumbled.

Mom's furrowed brow jumped out at me like the boogeyman who used to live under my bed. The confusion on her face and the butterflies in my stomach made me feel like I was going to explode, and I burst into tears and told her I needed to share some news with her.

"Sit down," she said calmly, but her Worried Mom look told me she was anxious and concerned as we sat down to talk.

"I'm pregnant," I said. I looked down at the ball of damp sheets in my arms so I didn't have to look into her eyes. I couldn't bear to see her disappointment because the weight of my own was already suffocating me.

"Oh, Tracy," she said, and I waited for what would come next. Those next few seconds felt like hours, and my mind raced as I tried to predict whether her words would be laced with anger, sadness, or embarrassment.

"Those next few seconds felt like hours, and my mind raced as I tried to predict whether her words would be laced with anger, sadness, or embarrassment."

"Is this why you decided to stay home and attend college here?" she asked, her tone of voice hard to read. "Did you know you were pregnant when you made that decision?"

It wasn't the reason, and after I answered her question, I didn't say much else. The news was still so fresh for me, I didn't yet know what would come next. Would I live at home and raise my baby under Mom and Dad's roof, or would I be a young bride? Would I be able to juggle school, a job, and a new baby when I could barely take care of myself? And could I add a husband to that juggling act when I had no idea how to be a wife? My mind was spinning nonstop with the what-ifs.

"Let's keep this to ourselves today," my mom finally said. "It's your dad's birthday." She didn't say, "Don't ruin your dad's birthday," but I knew that's what she meant.

I know other women who also got pregnant at a young age. While it was not part of their plan either, it was different for me. It was worse. It was embarrassing. It was absolutely against the rules—which I usually followed closely—in my large, Catholic family.

I now realize those rules were part of my life's checklist—a checklist I began when I was a little girl. There was a certain way to do things, and any other way wasn't part of the checklist.

What was on the list? Good grades. Home by curfew. Follow in my older siblings' impressive footsteps. A college degree. Marriage. Kids. And all in that order.

My dad owned a local grocery store—passed down from his dad and, before that, his grandpa—in our small hometown. I was known as one of the younger Bahn kids, seventh in a line of eight.

I felt there were unspoken expectations of me, as part of that lineup of kids in a family of small business owners in an even smaller town. I remember near the end of my junior year of high school, when I got my senior class schedule approved, and the guidance counselor asked why I didn't want to take physics, the senior-level science class.

"Your brother and sisters took it. You can take it, too." The end of that story? Physics ended up on my senior class schedule.

Now, I have to admit, it wasn't a terrible class, and I don't have permanent scarring from the lessons on electromagnetism. That came later, when I reflected on how much of my life centered around my fear of bucking the system. For years, I'd played by the rules and followed that perfect checklist.

I'd always felt the need to color inside the lines of life, and yet there were so many times my crayons went way beyond those boundaries.

I looked at those times as failures, so I'd scoot myself back inside the lines because that's what I was "supposed" to do. And yet each time, a pull—almost a magnetic force—would draw me right back out where I wanted to be.

The checklist life was familiar. It was expected. And it was stifling.

When I made the decision to ramp up my self-awareness, I began to see that the checklist life prevented me from being my authentic self. I lived a "have to" life rather than a "get to" life. And it was time to change that.

QUESTION TO CONSIDER
In what area(s) of your life do you stay within the lines but wish you could joyously color anywhere you want? *

ACTION TO IMPLEMENT
Start a Checklist Chart
- Each time you feel yourself move in a direction that feels mandatory rather than enjoyable, add it to your list.
- Next to each item on your list, create a way to make your choice gratifying and enjoyable rather than obligatory.

_____

_____

_____

_____

_____

_____

_____

_____

CHAPTER 2

Stop the Box Checking

> *"When I discover who I am, I'll be free."*
> —RALPH ELLISON, INVISIBLE MAN

t's funny how life works. Without any conscious effort, we create our checklist for life and then decide at some point that it's not enjoyable. The life we've created feels monotonous rather than marvelous.

Such was the case for my friend-turned-client, Cathy. People saw her as a superwoman—and for a long time, she saw herself that way, too. Over the course of her career, she built several successful businesses from the ground up. She and her husband have five children, and she is a regular volunteer for various organizations.

Yes, Cathy can juggle a lot of balls. But one day those balls tumbled down on top of her, and she met me at a coffee shop with tear-filled eyes.

"I don't know what's wrong with me," she said, "but it's time to put up my white surrender flag. I just can't do this anymore. I look at my life and see that I have everything I ever wanted: marriage, large family, dream business, community involvement. I have the life I used to visualize for myself and never thought I would be able to have."

"I'm sorry," I said. "I thought you said there's something wrong. If you have your dream life, what's the issue?"

> **"I don't know what's wrong with me," she said, "but it's time to put up my white surrender flag."**

"The issue," she said as tears rolled down her face, "is that I have my dream life, and I hate it. More days than not, that dream I once pictured feels more like a nightmare. And then I add to it and make it worse. Mike and I talked about becoming foster parents, and I have a new business venture that just fell into my lap. It's like I can't stop the ride even though I'm the one in the driver's seat."

The checklist life we fall into deceives us. We check off those boxes and tell ourselves we do it all well—whatever "it" is. That's what life is supposed to be, right? Get the things done—ALL the things—and then happiness and contentment will follow.

Here's a question to ponder: when you finish all the things, do you feel happy and content, or do you go out and find more to add to the checklist?

When we stop the cycle of box checking, we make a conscious choice to do life in a different way. Cathy decided to do just that. She found a way to stop the ride—the box checking—and she simplified her life. She declined the new business venture, put the idea of being a foster parent on the back burner, and reduced her volunteer commitments. She delegated tasks in her business that she'd always insisted she had to do herself and noticed how good it felt to slow down.

She moved from an outlook of quantity—living life like it was a race to be won—to one of quality, where she found what mattered most to her. She also learned something important about herself—something she loved but had never given herself before. She gifted herself with quiet time. Time to take a walk on a nearby hiking trail. Time to sit in a coffee shop and write in her journal. Time to listen to the songs the birds sang as she relaxed on her patio.

I related to Cathy because I'd lived so many years of my life checking all the boxes on my checklist. I liked to feel needed but then felt suffocated when I couldn't keep up with everything. It was a strange game of tug-of-war I played. The world wasn't out to get me as I once thought. I did it to myself.

When my kids were in junior high and high school, I took night classes after work. My classes ended at 9 p.m., then I'd drive the seventy-five minutes home. My checklist had such a hold on me at that time that when I'd arrive home after 10 p.m., I'd still go to our basement and lift weights or jog on the treadmill because, well, that was part of my day. It had nothing to do with the mental or physical health benefits I might achieve. It was all about the checklist.

At the time I saw myself as dedicated and disciplined. I had a workout on the checklist, and I was the checklist queen. Can't skip it if it's on the checklist, right?

The irony of that state I was in? I spent so much time committed to those checks on my checklist, I didn't tune in to the fact that my kids were growing up. They wouldn't be around forever. They'd become adults and live their own lives one day. Enough time has passed to have made that realization a reality, and I look now at that completed checklist and realize it has little meaning for me.

Cathy, a faster learner than I, now homeschools her kids while employees take care of most of her business responsibilities. Her checklist life is a thing of the past, and she continues to live version 2.0 of her dream life.

QUESTION TO CONSIDER
In what parts of your life are you too focused on your checklist, and what can you do to change that?

ACTION TO IMPLEMENT
Track the Monotony
- For one week, keep a log of how you spend your time.
- At the end of the week, review the log and highlight the activities that fill your heart with joy, excitement, and pride.
- Make a commitment to yourself to increase the frequency of those activities over the next month.

_____

_____

_____

_____

_____

_____

_____

CHAPTER 3

Lead with Pride

"If you so choose, every mistake can lead to greater understanding and effectiveness. If you so choose, every frustration can help you to be more patient and more persistent."
—RALPH MARSTON

In my family, we didn't talk about emotions. Did we experience a wide array of them? Of course! Remember, there were ten of us under one roof!

From love, contentment, joy, and acceptance to boredom, fear, frustration, and anger, I'd say you could have thrown a dart at a board of emotions and hit one that someone in our house felt at any given moment. We didn't talk about them, though.

My parents were hard workers who provided an incredible childhood for my siblings and me. Could I tell when Mom was having a stressful day? Sure. As a mother of eight kids, did she experience a lot of stress? Absolutely! And yet, we didn't talk about it. It was just there. It floated in the air like the smoke that lingers when a lit match is added to a pile of wet leaves.

I learned by example to work hard and create my own happy, but I didn't learn what to do when the emotion I felt was more often frustration than it was joy. The cause of my frustration wasn't something I could pinpoint through many of my adult years, but now I know what it was. It was the frustration of my checklist life and the constraint I felt as a result.

My hometown is considered by some to be a modern-day Mayberry. Several generations of families live here. One public school system. No stoplights. No big businesses. It's a place where everyone knows your name.

Back in the late eighties, my small Illinois community hosted the first-ever Tour de Donut bike race. That first year, twenty-five participants entered the thirty-plus-mile race. Fast forward three decades, and now there are close to two thousand people who come from all over the country to ride in it. The name of the event, of course, is a spoof of the prestigious Tour de France, and the participants who enter the race can be categorized into two main groups.

Group One is made up of the serious bike racers. They come with their team. They wear biking gear. And they're committed to pedaling thirty-four miles of hilly terrain in the July heat and humidity.

Group Two is made up of the people who may not finish those thirty-four miles the fastest, but who tuned in to that fabulous word in the name of the race—donut! You see, for each donut a rider eats at any of the stops along the bike route, five minutes are shaved off that rider's final time.

About ten years ago, my time wasn't as consumed as it once was with my kids' activities, and I decided I wanted to get more involved in community events. I thought about the Tour de Donut and didn't have faith that I could ride all those sweltering, hilly miles. I also knew a breakfast of multiple donuts wasn't the healthiest option, so I decided to compromise and volunteer to help with the event.

My volunteer job was simple. I walked out my front door at 6:30 a.m. one Saturday in July, commuted across the street to the community park where the race began, and then distributed shirts to the race participants.

When a participant told us the shirts ran smaller/larger/wider/narrower/redder/bluer than they expected, we were to smile and let them know they could check back in after the race to see if their preferred shirt was available. On average, fifty percent or more of those who were given shirts from our volunteer team wanted a different one.

For a mere three hours per year, though, the job was easy to manage. Or it was until the year Kelly showed up as a volunteer on our team. She arrived thirty minutes late for our shift and then groaned, "Ugh, where's the coffee?"

"No coffee here," another volunteer answered. "They've got some water over there, though."

"You're kidding, right?" Kelly whined. "They expect us to be here at the butt crack of dawn, and then they don't even provide caffeine for the volunteers?"

As participants came to our stand to get their shirts, most of our volunteer team smiled, wished them good luck, and thanked them for their presence at our event. Kelly, on the other hand, kept that scowl on her face, and no kind words came from her mouth.

That first year with Kelly was uncomfortable for me. I couldn't believe she didn't understand that the way we show up at that little T-shirt stand is a representation of not only who we are as individuals, but also what our community is all about.

I said nothing to Kelly about her rude comments to participants. I just went home after my shift with a bad taste in my mouth.

The second year she came was the year a participant pushed back and told Kelly he'd paid for a shirt that would fit, and he wouldn't take no for an answer. Yes, that was the year Kelly moved from inferior customer service to atrocious customer service.

"You see this word on the back of my shirt?" she asked. "It says 'Volunteer.' I don't get paid to be here. I don't care what size shirt you want. Now get out of the #$@& way so I can get the next guy's shirt."

The feelings I'd felt the year before escalated from confusion and embarrassment to anger.

Why didn't I speak up when Kelly showed such disrespect? Oh yes, now I remember. It's because I like to follow rules. Rule followers don't make waves. They follow what they're used to and put blinders on when things don't follow the well-traveled path. My checklist was a lifelong follower of that path.

> **❝Rule followers don't make waves. They follow what they're used to and put blinders on when things don't follow the well-traveled path.❞**

My commitment to support my community remained, and I made a decision to show up again the following year. Kelly was part of our team again, although I couldn't figure out why she continued to volunteer. The T-shirts, I knew, would again be too small/big/wide/narrow/red/

blue. There was something different that year, though. That year I brought an up-leveled mindset with me.

When an un-caffeinated Kelly showed up and complained for the third year in a row, I suggested she walk down the block to a convenience store and get some coffee. When she returned, the caffeine had already begun working its magic, so I went further.

"Hey, everyone," I said. "You know how we always stumble over each other when we get busy? How about if we switch things up this year? Three of us can take the shirt orders, and the other two can stand by the shirts and toss the sizes needed to those of us up front."

Kelly spoke up first. "Do you all care if I stand back by the shirts and deliver them? You might not have noticed this about me, but I'm not much of a people person."

Our process that year was smoother than it had ever been. And the next year Kelly showed up with coffee in hand and stated that she'd like to work with the shirts and not the customers once again.

My lesson learned from that Tour de Donut experience? When I let go of the comfort of my checklist—that fear of a new and different route—I emerge as the leader I am. And those emotions of confusion, embarrassment, and anger make a huge shift to those of confidence, empowerment, and pride.

QUESTION TO CONSIDER
**What emotions don't serve you well?
What are the thoughts that bring about
those emotions?**

ACTION TO IMPLEMENT
Take Control of Those Emotions
- Think of an emotion you consider to be negative.
- Write the thoughts that bring about that feeling for you.
  - For example, *I feel fearful when I think about experiencing a horrible rejection.*
- Take a deep breath and feel the emotion, fighting the urge to push it away.
- Continue taking deep breaths, and recognize that you're safe—even when you feel this emotion.

CHAPTER 4

_____

_____

_____

_____

_____

_____

Build the Belief

"Believe something and the Universe is on its way to being changed."
—DIANE DUANE, SO YOU WANT TO BE A WIZARD

To see is to believe, right? It's what we've always been taught. You see the proof, and then you build your belief around it.

Wrong! In my coach certification program, I learned that our belief about belief is backwards. And by backwards, I mean a shift of a hundred and eighty degrees is needed to understand the full power of belief.

When we turn it around, we get this: to believe is to see. My client Analise's story is a perfect example of this mantra.

Analise has a life many would call picture perfect. She has a husband who adores her and three children—ages seven, nine, and seventeen—who are the center of her world. Analise's dad lives practically next door, and a permanent path worn down by the kids connects their houses.

She is a successful CPA with a thriving practice, due in part to her unique approach to what many see as a super dull job. Because of that approach and her original programs, her small business clients not only benefit from her exceptional accounting skills; they also gain valuable knowledge about how to make their business revenue work for them in the most effective ways.

Now I realize that picture does sound quite perfect, but it wasn't always that way. Analise lost her mother when she was six years old, so she was raised by her dad alone. They were close until she told him he would be a grandfather when she was just sixteen years old. That news was too much for him to bear, and in swift fashion, Analise was kicked out of the house.

Over the past eighteen years, Analise did struggle with belief. Belief that she'd be a good mom. Belief that she would always love her first boyfriend and build an incredible life with him. Belief that she'd ever get to college, let alone finish high school. Belief that one day she'd again have a strong relationship with her dad. Belief in herself.

Analise, like most of us, grew up thinking that to see is to believe. When she moved in with her boyfriend's family at the age of sixteen with a baby on the way and a history test to study for, all she saw was the death of the life she once dreamed she'd have. She couldn't see her way out of her predicament. Analise believed in a life full of struggle and pain because that's all she could see.

Analise eventually did understand that to believe is to see. As a young mother, she focused her thoughts on what she wanted to achieve and didn't allow obstacles to get in her way.

Webster defines the word *belief* as something that is accepted, considered to be true, or held as an opinion. I view a belief as a thought that we think over and over again until it forms a permanent imprint on our soul.

I didn't believe I could create a successful business where I was able to help women say no to a checklist life and yes to their best life, so I continued to play it safe and live a checklist life. The thoughts that ran on repeat in my head went something like this:

You have bills to pay.
Be an adult and suck it up.
People do what they have to do every day.
When retirement comes, you'll get to do what you want.
The rest of the world has figured out how to live this checklist life, so buck up and figure it out.

Those thoughts played in my brain over and over, much like the playlists I'd record as a pre-teen on those treasured cassette tapes (Air Supply, anyone?).

The thing is, the more I played those mixtapes of thoughts, the more I believed them. And the more I believed them, the more I remained stuck.

> **❝In order to get unstuck, in order to throw my checklist away, in order to create that business so I could help other women throw their checklists away, I needed to change my thoughts.❞**

In order to get unstuck, in order to throw my checklist away, in order to create that business so I could help other women throw their checklists away, I needed to change my thoughts. I needed thoughts that would serve me. I needed thoughts like:

I live an abundant life.

My life is filled to the brim with "get to" opportunities.

I am a powerful decision maker who lives with certainty.

I am privileged to help women throw their checklist lives away.

When I made the powerful decision to change my thoughts, I also changed my beliefs. Once my new and improved beliefs were in place, I began to see the positive changes in my life. And now I share my new mantra— to believe is to see—with others who are ready to throw away their checklists.

QUESTION TO CONSIDER
What negative thoughts do you repeatedly think? What would you prefer to think?

ACTION TO IMPLEMENT
Believe It to See It

- Make a list of thoughts that serve you well. For instance:

  I am a good person.

  People need what I have to share.

  I am an expert in what I do.

  I show up with certainty and confidence wherever I go.

- Choose one or two thoughts from your list to focus on every day.
- Play those positive "cassette tapes" often so that those thoughts become beliefs.

CHAPTER 5

Live in a New Neighborhood

"Authenticity is a collection of choices that we make every day. It's about the choice to show up and be real. The choice to be honest. The choice to let our true selves be seen."
—*BRENÉ BROWN*

One thing our brains do well is keep us safe. They don't like it when we jump into unfamiliar territory, and they work hard to keep us comfortable and secure. Checklists in life accomplish the same result.

When we stick to the expectations listed on our checklist, we stay in the same "neighborhood" we've always known. The neighborhood includes the smell of fresh-cut lawns, the sound of kids' laughter, the feeling of a pat on the back from longtime neighborhood friends, and the taste of neighbor JoAnn's homemade cookies. It's all . . . fine. It's familiar and comfortable and safe and fine.

And when we decide we'd rather have life-changing than fine, we realize it's a whole lot easier to stay with what we know than try to reinvent the wheel (or in this example, the neighborhood).

My client Beth wanted to throw away her checklist for good when we began our work.

"I should be happy," she told me. "I have a good marriage, wonderful kids, and a business I love, but something feels off. You don't know the real me yet, but that's because I've kept her hidden for so long. The Beth I was before was straightforward and outspoken. I stood up for who I was and what I believed in and didn't give a hoot what others thought of my opinions."

As Beth continued, I learned that when she got married and became a mother, she silenced her inner matter-of-fact maven and instead went along with what others wanted. She acquiesced to her husband's viewpoints on where to live, how to raise their children, and even what to make for dinner. As her children grew, she succumbed to their wants and needs. Even at work, where she was the CEO, she agreed with whatever her leadership team suggested without any pushback or request for additional information before making a final decision.

It was easy to see Beth was frustrated and sad. "Last week I thought I'd lose it one day at work when I pushed back a bit at the direction my team lead wanted to take. I spoke up, and he dismissed my opinion. I've been silent so long it's like people don't even realize it's my name on the door!"

I knew our work would involve Beth's search for the person she once was—her authentic self. That was the missing piece in her life. I also sensed that she'd fallen so far into her checklist life—a life where she lived as the person she felt she was supposed to be—she didn't have faith she'd even be able to show up as her true self.

We worked together over several months, and Beth felt empowered when she showed up in a more genuine, true-to-herself way. "It feels so good to be the real me," she said one day.

As she became more comfortable and shared her opinions—even when they weren't the most popular opinions—Beth noticed another change. Her friends distanced themselves, and she was no longer invited to join them for hikes and lunches and shopping. She and her husband argued more than ever. And her relationships with her kids and work team were also on shaky ground.

Even with all that discord, she knew she wouldn't go back to the meek woman she'd lived as for so many years. She felt free and confident when she spoke her mind, and as her inner circle began to dissipate, she reacted by asserting herself even more. The Beth who had worn a mask of compliance for so long became like a tiger let out of its cage who wouldn't be restrained again.

Beth's world resisted when she showed up as her true, no-checklist self.

> **❝Beth's world resisted when she showed up as her true, no-checklist self.❞**

Remember how our brain likes to keep us safe? And that neighborhood we've lived in our whole life? For Beth, that was the masked life she lived for many years. She was safe, comfortable, and fine. She knew all her neighbors and what to expect from them. When she decided to show up as the authoritative woman she is, she was in her glory, but those who spent time with her for years weren't quite sure who this woman was.

As her new self and old world continued to collide, Beth's onetime emotions of dissatisfaction and sadness turned to resentment and confusion. She'd say she could leave it all behind with no problem. And by "it," she meant everyone—her husband, kids, coworkers, and friends. But that wasn't the answer to her woes.

My work with Beth at this point involved helping her look through a new lens to see how she could have the best of both worlds. She continued to share her opinions with others. She also learned to tailor her communication to invite people into it, rather than push them out. Over time, her relationships improved, and she lived her life mask- and checklist-free.

I don't want to give our brains a bad rap. When they pull us back to the familiarity and comfort of what we've always done, they do their job. They want to keep us safe. Our job, then, is to override what the brain tells us at times so we can live as the genuine, authentic person we are.

QUESTION TO CONSIDER
In what sheltered neighborhood do you live? What would you like to change about that norm?

ACTION TO IMPLEMENT
Reconstruct Your Neighborhood
- Generate two lists: My Current Neighborhood and My Future Neighborhood.
- Tune in to the differences between the two lists.
- Devise a plan to move yourself from the neighborhood that keeps you stuck, to the neighborhood that lights you up!

_____

_____

_____

_____

_____

CHAPTER 6

Mix in Some Self-Care

"Self-care is how you take your power back."
—*LALAH DELIA*

elf-care is a term that hasn't been around all that
long. My mom didn't discuss her need for self-care,
and even as a young woman myself, I heard friends
discuss their desire for more sleep or their goal to exercise
more, but we didn't go much deeper than that. The actual
term is considered by many to be a buzzword, and its
meaning can cause confusion.

I view self-care as a way to listen to myself and use
what I hear to care for my mind, body, and spirit. That
could mean more sleep each night and a more consistent
exercise routine. For me, it also includes time to focus on
stories I tell myself that don't serve me well, a practice of

forgiveness and acceptance, and time with people who make me belly laugh.

When I was raising my kids, I can't say I ever took time to focus on my self-care. I was too wrapped up in what we'd have for dinner so we could get to our various evening events, who needed which uniform washed by the next day, and what work projects needed time and attention. I was hyper-focused on my checklist and didn't give any thought to self-care.

Years later, after my kids were grown, I met Alyssa. I saw my past self in her, and I believe we got along so well because I felt nostalgic as I watched her run at top speed on the hamster wheel of life. Between our kids, husbands, pets, jobs, and events and obligations for all of the above, we both earned memberships in the Get It All Done Club. That club, however, didn't focus any time or attention on how we cared for ourselves.

Alyssa worked in a cutthroat industry, one that valued long work days over reasonable hours that would have allowed her to spend more time with her family. Her work days were filled with meeting after meeting, so she did a good portion of her work after the kids went to bed and often didn't go to bed herself until 1:30 or 2:00 a.m., only to start again at 5:30 or 6:00 a.m.

I saw Alyssa and her daughter in a coffee shop one Saturday morning, and we caught up on each other's family and work happenings. She shared the many challenges she faced at work while her daughter enjoyed her cinnamon roll, one fluffy layer at a time.

"What do you want to be when you grow up?" I asked the young girl.

"Hmm…I don't know," she said, and then she sat up straight and declared, "but I know one thing—I don't want to be a leader!" Cue the jaw drop from her mother, leader of her department.

From her daughter's viewpoint, that answer made perfect sense. I guessed Alyssa's frustrations about work weren't only made apparent with me that morning. When our bucket of frustration overflows, that runoff spills into many areas of our life.

This meant when Alyssa had a day of meetings where nothing got accomplished, her frustration at her kids, who hadn't started homework before she arrived home, was amplified. An extra-inning baseball game where her son was the star pitcher could send her into a tailspin of impatience and annoyance. And a week of 3 a.m. bedtimes because the kids decided to tag-team the flu resulted in a wife, mother, and leader who was so exhausted she broke down in tears at the most inopportune times.

So where's the self-care when our checklist repels any healthy habits we want to implement? We tell ourselves we don't have time to get more sleep, exercise on a regular basis, or refill our water bottles with the recommended number of ounces. We're too busy with the work involved in the achievement of those precious checkmarks.

❝So where's the self-care when our checklist repels any healthy habits we want to implement?❞

But once the dog gets his shots, the laundry is clean, the lunches are made, the work is as finished as it will be today, the bills are paid, and we put our head on the pillow, is it enough to say that at least our checklist looks good? My answer is a firm no.

I learned that self-care isn't selfish. It's selfless. It's the whole oxygen mask lesson that flight attendants share with us when the plane is about to take off. We've got to put on our own before we can help others.

Self-care is the antidote to a checklist life because when we take care of the woman who gets it all done, we show up as the mom they'll never forget for all the right reasons, the professional who kills it in her presentations to top clients, and the wife he looks at with the same sparkle in his eye he had when she walked down the aisle many years ago.

QUESTION TO CONSIDER
How do you already practice self-care each day? How can you incorporate more?

ACTION TO IMPLEMENT
Design Your Self-Care Plan

- Make a list of everything in your current self-care routine.
- Remove any items on the list that are no longer bringing you joy, peace, or fulfillment.
- Add any new self-care items you'd like to implement.
- Commit to implementing a minimum of one self-care item from your list every day.

CHAPTER 7

Give Yourself Some Grace

"I do not at all understand the mystery of grace—only that it meets us where we are but does not leave us where it found us."
—ANNE LAMOTT

Grace. **It's not something** I've ever given much thought; that is, I didn't think about it until I hired my first coach. If I had a nickel for every time he told me in his calm voice, "Tracy, you've got to give yourself some grace," I'd have far too many nickels to count!

I wasn't a "give yourself some grace" kind of girl. I was a "gotta get it done" girl. And the more I got done, the more I added to my checklist. I was so tuned in to the "right" way to do things that even now, when I say, "get it done," I hear the echo of nuns from my youth: "Tracy, young girls don't get things done. The turkey we've cooked is done. Young girls get things finished."

Seems like such a silly thing to remember, but when I dig deep, I realize the reason it's so clear in my mind is because I didn't like to be called out like that. I didn't appreciate constructive criticism, and when I received it, I sure didn't give myself any grace!

Madeline, a coach I connected with a few years ago, was also on the No Grace Bus for a while. I've always coached clients through the company I started. Madeline, however, coached people through her employer. She was part of their people development department. In addition to being an expert in what she did, she also believed it was the perfect job for her.

That is, until the day her world turned upside down and her company made the decision to eliminate Madeline's position. On her last day of employment, she was thanked for her service, made aware of the severance package she would receive, and told to clean out her desk.

To say this was a complete surprise to Madeline is an understatement. "I was numb when I heard the news. It felt like time stood still as I recovered from the shock of the announcement," she told me.

She left work that day unsure of what came next. After some much-deserved time to collect her thoughts and focus on a game plan, Madeline made the decision to start her own coaching business. She knew she was a good coach and felt she was ready to be the owner of the next stage of her career.

The road to business success wasn't easy. I remember our conversation several weeks into her new venture when she told me, "I'm so stuck on the why behind the company's decision to wipe out my position. Why would they make a decision like that? How will their employees continue to learn and grow so they can provide the best service to their clients?"

She couldn't get over the demise of her former life. It was a checklist life, and one she enjoyed. She had been so . . . comfortable.

While one part of her life wouldn't stop—those swirling thoughts—another part wouldn't get started. Madeline had no clients to serve. She didn't consider herself to be an outgoing person and therefore didn't attend networking events. The thought of them made her anxious, and in her mind the downside far outweighed the upside.

"Wouldn't it be great," she said one day, "if clients just showed up at the front door and asked me to be their coach?"

I had to agree that would be marvelous, but, of course, the clients didn't come to her front door, and her "why me" thoughts continued to spin in her mind. The money from her severance package didn't reproduce on its own. Madeline needed to make some changes. Fast.

"It's time for me to let it go," she told me one day.

"What do you mean?" I asked.

"My last job was such a good experience for me, but it's over now. I need to move on. I left my workplace in the physical sense a few months ago, and now I need to leave it from a mental and emotional standpoint, too."

Madeline knew it was time to give herself some grace.

She understood people and knew how to help them live their best life through the coaching she provided. She resolved to push through the discomfort of being a salesperson, and she attended networking events. She wrote articles in her areas of specialty and was invited to be a guest on podcasts where her ideal clients were in the audience.

As Madeline shed her former checklist life, she created a new life for herself—one that included work she loved, clients to serve, and an attitude of gratitude and grace.

> **❝Our checklist becomes part of who we are. It is an unconscious piece of us, like background noise we don't even notice.❞**

Our checklist becomes part of who we are. It is an unconscious piece of us, like background noise we don't even notice. It's often painful to strip away that checklist life. It feels unfair and uncomfortable. When we push through the discomfort and give ourselves some much-needed grace, we win at this thing called life.

QUESTION TO CONSIDER
In what areas of your life could you give
yourself more grace?

ACTION TO IMPLEMENT
Add Grace

- Focus on the areas of your life where you're hard
  on yourself.
- Formulate strategies to allow yourself more
  grace in those areas. For instance:
  - Are all those areas/tasks/responsibilities still
    needed, or can you eliminate some?
  - How can you add more love and grace to
    the way you talk to yourself about those
    specific areas?

CHAPTER 8

Paint Your Masterpiece

"Your life is your canvas, and you are the masterpiece. There are a million ways to be kind, amazing, fabulous, creative, bold, and interesting."

—KERLI

In my mind, my life is a masterpiece that I create each and every day. I get to choose what's in the masterpiece, and my choices aren't predetermined based on a list I follow.

When I was immersed in my checklist life, my canvas was more like a paint-by-number picture with the colors all pre-planned. I'd complete a task or life event and add a check mark to the checklist that dictated my life plan.

My friend Sandra lived that same paint-by-number life for many years, and she adored it. Her husband was a successful businessman who earned a multiple six-figure income, and Sandra was comfortable in her role as a stay-at-home-mom to their two children.

When her kids were thirteen and fifteen, Sandra decided to go back to school to further her education. Her intention was less about a degree in a particular field and more about her goal to learn something new each day and keep her mind active in the process. Her school-work along with her regular responsibilities challenged her, but she stuck with it. She enjoyed her life and all it offered her.

As Sandra continued her studies semester by semester, she became more and more puzzled by her husband's questions about what she'd like to do when she earned her degree. He wasn't direct with his questions but rather slid in sly comments every chance he got.

"That's great that you enjoy your history class so much. What do you think about teaching?" he asked her one day. "I could see you in a classroom with a group of kids. Maybe high school history. What do you think?"

"It was funny," Sandra told me as she shared their conversation with me. "I just laughed at his suggestion because I found it to be ridiculous. My classes are more for fun than anything else. I don't have plans to get a full-time job. Sure, the kids are more self-sufficient now, but I'm still the one who cooks, cleans, does the laundry, and manages transportation. It's a lot to keep up with, and I can't imagine if I had to add a job to the mix."

Sandra knew her husband supported her decision to go to college and was grateful they were in a position to be able to afford her classes and her role as a stay-at-home mom. Her life was all she'd ever hoped for. She was active, comfortable, and joyful.

That joy and comfort ceased when she learned of her husband's affair. The news came to her from a friend who saw Sandra's husband out with another woman. He and the young woman who worked for him held hands and kissed over the table. There was no way to mistake their time together for anything work-related. As the words floated from her friend's mouth to Sandra's ears, she felt the oxygen leave her lungs.

Sandra believed marriage was for life, and the word divorce had never been in her vocabulary. She suggested they go to a counselor, but was shocked to hear her husband didn't want to salvage the marriage. He wanted a divorce. And he didn't want to support an ex-wife who didn't have a job.

Sandra's view of her life changed faster than she ever could have imagined. One day she looked through the windshield at her comfortable life as a wife, mother, and student, and the next she was panicked as she looked in the rear-view mirror at the life she would leave behind. How would she make it as a single mom? It was so far from the world she'd lived in for so long.

We got together a couple of months after her husband moved out of their house and in with his mistress. "I'm numb," she told me. "I go through the motions every day. The kids still need me to be that mom who has their meals, laundry, and ride ready to go, but I barely function otherwise."

She stayed committed to her studies because she'd started the semester and wasn't one to give up on anything she set out to do (and the irony of that wasn't lost on her). She moved through life not by choice but by necessity. Until one day she decided to change that.

Divorce proceedings moved along, and it was agreed that her ex would pay child support for three years until their youngest turned eighteen. She'd also receive spousal support for those three years. After that she was on her own, and not just from a financial standpoint. She also knew it was up to her to stay strong emotionally for her kids and herself.

For a long time, Sandra viewed her husband's affair as something that happened *to* her. It was the proverbial rug that was pulled out from under her that destroyed the remarkable life she had lived.

It took time—and some coaching—for Sandra to realize life is a masterpiece we have the opportunity to create. Sometimes we start a beautiful painting on the canvas of life, and after a while, we realize the color scheme or the design isn't what we want anymore.

"Sometimes we start a beautiful painting on the canvas of life, and after a while, we realize the color scheme or the design isn't what we want anymore."

The most incredible thing about it is that we can change our original masterpiece anytime we choose to do so. I changed mine when I threw my checklist life away. And Sandra changed hers when she moved from victim to victor and in the process became an even more incredible mother and friend.

QUESTION TO CONSIDER
What would you like to change about the masterpiece you've begun to create?

ACTION TO IMPLEMENT
Get to Work on Your Canvas
- Create a dream list of twenty accomplishments you'd like to achieve.
- Read your list every day.
- Focus on the energy you feel as you accomplish items on the list, and use that energy as inspiration to continue the completion of your life canvas.

_____

_____

_____

_____

_____

_____

_____

CHAPTER 9

Squash the Shame

"There is no shame in beginning again, for you get a chance to build bigger and better than before."
—LEON BROWN

I used to think shame and guilt were synonymous. Then I watched the great Brené Brown's TED Talk, "Listening to Shame," and I was enlightened.

Brown says, "Shame is a focus on self; guilt is a focus on behavior. Shame is, 'I am bad.' Guilt is, 'I did something bad.'"

It was a revelation for me. That was the moment I realized the pervasiveness of shame in my life.

My checklist lost its order when I was eighteen and pregnant, and went a step further six weeks after Dad's birthday when I married the father of my baby. By then I had started my second semester of college at a local university.

When I went to class on the Monday after my Saturday wedding, I listened as other college freshmen discussed their crazy weekend antics.

"Did you go to that party? It was insane! So much fun!"

I waited for class to begin and didn't join in the conversation. I thought—but didn't share—*I got married over the weekend. I'm a wife. I'll be a mom in six months.*

The predominant feeling that swirled within me was shame.

I thought, *I am bad. I did something wrong. I won't ever go to any college parties. I'm a wife now. I need to cook and clean and do the laundry.*

I pushed the shame down and focused on my checklist for what came next.

Fast forward three years, and I earned my bachelor's degree in elementary education. The diploma wasn't the only thing I gained, though. Now there were two babies.

My second son was born the summer before my last semester of college. My most important semester, where I taught, planned, and managed a classroom under my mentor teacher's guidance, was also the time I learned to juggle two kids and a household.

The strangest thing about this time in my life? I didn't think it was strange at all. My checklist filled up faster than most, and I built a wall around myself to hide the shame I felt inside.

ff My checklist filled up faster than most, and I built a wall around myself to hide the shame I felt inside. ff

When I met people who commented on my age (I was twenty-one) and my young family, I didn't reply with kindness, compassion, and gratitude. The wall I'd built didn't allow for those types of responses. I kept the shame inside and did my best to maintain a tough "none of your business" exterior while I continued to check off those boxes.

My third child was born during the last two weeks of my first year as a teacher. Three kids in just under five years. The summer my youngest turned five, I earned my master's degree. I worked my checklist like a pro, to say the least.

Some would have put up their surrender flag at this point, but not me. I didn't know where I was headed on my road beyond my master's degree. I just knew it was important to keep up with the checkmarks on my checklist of life.

I taught for twelve years and enjoyed much of my time in the classroom. At this time, my kids were in their teen and pre-teen years, and much to my dismay, they weren't as interested in time with Mom as they once were. I felt restless. It was as if I examined my checklist and saw, at the age of thirty-four, I'd almost run out of boxes to check. I felt the need to create new ones. I was ready for a change.

I've always loved to learn and attend school, so I decided to begin court reporting school, a career that would allow for flexibility in my schedule. It seemed like a smart decision, given the many activities my kids were involved in and my desire to be there to root them on. I attended classes at night and taught by day, and then worked at a legal services business as an administrative assistant for a handful of hours that summer.

With just a few weeks of summer left, the owner of the business asked me to continue there on a full-time basis. I was eager for a change, but others in my life weren't quite as enthusiastic.

I remember my mom's words. "Oh, Tracy. You worked so hard on your education. Does it make sense to move on to something else now?"

I couldn't put it into words. On one hand I felt anxious and fearful, and on the other hand I was curious and invigorated.

I wasn't able to explain it at the time, but when I look back now, I realize this was the start of my journey to a checklist-free life, a life with less shame and no boxes to check.

QUESTION TO CONSIDER:
What shame lives within you?

ACTION TO IMPLEMENT
Eliminate the Shame Game

- Draw a timeline on a sheet of paper and divide it into five-year increments.
- Add various pivotal memories you have—both positive and negative—for each increment on your timeline.
- As you reflect on your life as a whole, tune in to those times when shame was present.
- For any shame that still exists, create a plan to work through it:
  - What do you think about the shame you experience?
  - How do those thoughts make you feel?
  - What do you want to think instead?
  - What do you want to feel?
  - What actions can you take as a result of those desired thoughts and feelings?

_____

_____

_____

_____

CHAPTER 10

Create Your Tribe

"When we live in alignment with who we are and how we want to live, we will attract and find like-minded individuals."
—*AKIROQ BROST*

At a recent networking event, I had the great opportunity to hear former Major League Baseball pitcher Todd Stottlemyre speak. Now, I'll be honest, I didn't see it as a great opportunity prior to his presentation. Sports and I have never been the best of friends—I was the kid picked last for the kickball team, the baseball team, the wiffle ball team, and pretty much any other team that involved a ball and a great deal of coordination.

Due to that hate-hate relationship (and the shame I've always carried in my back pocket about my lack of athletic ability), I was pleasantly surprised to learn that

Mr. Stottlemyre is an expert speaker. He managed two important groups in his audience. His baseball fans were there to hear about how he pitched no-hitters and signed multi-million-dollar contracts. The rest of us were there to be inspired. And he didn't let either group down.

One of the lessons we were encouraged to follow was this one: avoid dream stealers. Perhaps you've never heard the term dream stealers, but it's easy to visualize those people, isn't it? You have a dream. You're excited to work toward the achievement of your dream. You put action steps in place to make your dream a reality. You move forward, and as each step is completed, you display it with pride on your dream stage.

And then a giant with feet the size of a Mack truck and a face that looks like your mom or your spouse or your coworker or your friend or your boss (you get the idea) comes onto your dream stage and demolishes what you've accomplished and any plans you have to continue on that path. Yep, those are your dream stealers.

Dream stealers like comfort and familiarity. They detest change and any plan to make a job, relationship, or life better. And because they don't make those changes in their own life, they also like to hold us back. They don't see change as a win. They fear it.

❝Dream stealers like comfort and familiarity. They detest change and any plan to make a job, relationship, or life better.❞

My client Chloe had always been a successful professional. She began her career in the finance industry, and when we began our work together, she was about to make a huge leap to a role in sales and marketing with a new organization. She was ecstatic about this change but noticed others in her inner circle didn't feel the same.

Chloe's husband didn't cheer her on. Instead, he questioned her every move. "Are you sure you'll be able to exceed the income you have now?"

Then came her mom's opinion. "Is now the right time for this? I thought you planned to start a family. That will be hard to do as you learn the ropes in a new industry."

Even her longtime friends came out of the woodwork with viewpoints. "But you've always been the numbers girl. Finance is where you belong. It will be hard to make this switch, don't you think?"

As the commentary continued, Chloe's excitement dwindled. She began to question herself and the decision she was about to make. Maybe they were right. Maybe this wasn't the right opportunity at the right time for the right money.

I watched the excitement dim in Chloe's eyes each week we met. The first time she shared her new venture with me, I saw her enthusiasm and heard it in all she shared. Over the course of just a few weeks, I watched her huge balloon of energy deflate little by little. The air continued to be released until her excitement was all but gone.

Chloe's dream stealers did their job, and she was wasn't even aware she'd helped them be successful.

"Who's in your tribe?" I asked her one day.

"My what?" she asked.

"Your tribe," I repeated. "You know, the people who just 'get' you. The ones who support you through thick and thin. The ones who cheer you on when you've made a big decision. The ones who continue to stand behind you no matter what gets in the way. Who are those people in your life?"

I saw the wheels turn in her head as she contemplated the question and then shared a few names with me.

"A tribe is so important when we face big life decisions," I told her. "People in your tribe keep your excitement up and your balloon inflated. They want nothing but the best for you."

One way to form a supportive tribe is to remove the dream stealers from our life. We don't need to be their Facebook friend or meet them every month for happy hour or get together with them and the kids at the playground. We get to choose who we spend our time with.

When it's a spouse, parent, or sibling who sucks the oxygen out of our fire, it's not always feasible to remove them from our life. Such was the case for Chloe. She did the work to set boundaries with those who acted as dream stealers in her life.

Chloe told her husband, mom, and friends that she didn't want to look backward to the job she used to have. If they wanted to do that, they could do so, but she wouldn't be part of it. She let them know she needed people who could be forward thinkers with her and for her. She knew her new adventure was the right move, and because of her conscious choice to move forward with the right support system—her tribe—she was able to enjoy this new stage in her career and life.

QUESTION TO CONSIDER:
How can you remove the dream stealers from your life and build a supportive tribe instead?

ACTION TO IMPLEMENT
Build Your Tribe One Person at a Time

- Make a list of the people in your life who support you, teach you, guide you, and are always in your corner.
- Next to each name, write how you've reciprocated support for that person.
- Commit to thanking the people in your tribe for who they are and how they help you.
- As you soak in more of the greatness that your tribe provides, your dream stealers will begin to fall away and out of your life. You will create a checklist-free life with no time or energy to give to the oxygen suckers (a.k.a. dream stealers)!

CHAPTER 11

Venture into Vulnerability

> *"To share your weakness is to make yourself vulnerable; to make yourself vulnerable is to show your strength."*
> —CRISS JAMI

didn't always know I was an introvert. For many years of my adult life, the now-common topic of introverts versus extroverts wasn't discussed. I've always known certain things about myself, though. For instance, I like to think about what to say before it comes out of my mouth. I hang out (some people say lurk) in Facebook groups for a while before I chime in. I prefer to socialize in small groups or one-on-one rather than at big parties or events, and when a large social get-together is a requirement, I schedule some alone time afterward to recharge my battery.

Yes, the verdict is in. My name is Tracy, and I am an introvert. I've put in a great deal of time and effort throughout my adult life to keep my thoughts and feelings to myself, and I let few in on what happens in my world.

This little feature of who I am at my core became apparent when I led a team of managers at the legal services business. Our company sponsored a two-day retreat where we learned from industry experts, discussed team goals, and developed strategies to achieve those goals. One of our activities was an assessment where we answered questions about our behavioral preferences, and then our team members answered questions about their perception of us.

My self-perception was that I liked to provide empathy to my team members for things that happened both in the workplace and out. If they had difficulties with an aging parent or a child who went to the principal's office on a regular basis, I wanted them to know those challenges were just as important to me as a client project or a deadline that would be difficult to make. I learned that my self-perception here was spot on. My entire team had answered questions that resulted in some meaningful feedback. I cared, and they knew I cared.

If we could have stopped there, I would have been golden, but instead we moved on to the next part—my team members' perception of me as a person. I had given myself high marks in how I showed up as a leader and how I shared personal morsels of who I am. My team, however, didn't agree. I learned they saw me as closed off, far too private, and even cool and aloof. I was dumbfounded. I cared so much about them and their personal and professional success. How could they not see that?

> **❝I learned they saw me as closed off, far too private, and even cool and aloof.❞**

As it turns out, I learned they did see that. They saw me give time, attention, compliments, and constructive feedback to them. The one thing I didn't give—and it was a big thing—was an awareness of who I was, what made me happy, what challenged me, and what happened in my world when I wasn't at work. I didn't understand their need for information like this, and it felt uncomfortable to think of how to share this. Then I realized I knew so much about them, while what they knew about me fit in a thimble.

I had missed the vulnerability needed to be the real me day in and day out. As I worked to be more vulnerable, it felt like I'd put on a pair of ice skates for a performance in the Winter Olympics. I laced up my skates, walked to the ice, and fell with my first step into the rink. Vulnerability felt uncertain, risky, and scary. It made me feel naked. It felt terrible and foreign.

Although it felt awful, it was just what I needed to make the changes to help me get to a better place. I baby stepped it for a while. I'd share tiny aspects of my personal life—a BBQ we hosted over the weekend, a great sale I found at a clothing store I knew one of my team members loved, a picture of my baby grandson's toothless grin. As I began to open up to my team, I noticed subtle changes. The level of trust between us increased. The ability to talk about difficult topics was easier. And a kind, compassionate look from across the conference room table became the norm when I shared my stories of challenges I faced.

Self-awareness is a gift. Involuntary self-awareness— the kind that comes when a team you love asks you to look in the mirror at yourself—is a gift that continues to give. It was my team's candid feedback that helped me realize I'd lived life in a bubble. My checklist was in the bubble with me, suffocating me. Vulnerability is how I popped the bubble and began a new, enlightened journey to the next stop in my life.

QUESTION TO CONSIDER:
What secrets live in your bubble? How can more vulnerability help you pop that bubble?

ACTION TO IMPLEMENT
Show 'Em the Real You

- Create a chart with three columns: Places I Go, People I See, and Thoughts I Have.
- In each column, list your most frequent places, people, and thoughts.
- Highlight every person, place, and thought where you find yourself holding back the real you.
- Under your chart, create thoughts that will help you show vulnerability so the world can celebrate the realness of who you are at your core.

_____

_____

_____

_____

_____

CHAPTER 12

Learn from the Best

> *"A mentor is someone who allows you to see the hope inside yourself."*
> —OPRAH WINFREY

My great fortune has been learning from several mentors throughout my life. Lucky for me, they all appeared exactly when I needed them most—some even appeared when I didn't think I needed them—and their guidance changed my life for the better.

In addition to what I've learned from mentors, I've also had the great opportunity to be a mentor for others, like my old acquaintance Melissa. I use the word acquaintance, but in reality, Melissa was ten years old the last time I'd seen her. I had been her fourth-grade teacher. We recently connected through social media and agreed to get together. I was eager to catch up on all that had happened since I'd last seen her in my classroom.

I remembered Melissa as a student who would finish her work and then ask if she could help others. She'd help them and would sometimes even help me with housekeeping tasks within the classroom. She always showed great compassion and respect to whoever she helped, and she committed to anything she put her mind to.

When we got together after all those years, I learned Melissa didn't lose any of her go-get-it nature. She owned a graphic design business where she created websites, logos, and print and digital ads for her clients. She started her business almost three years before with just three clients. At the time we got together, she worked with almost thirty.

"I love what I do," she told me. "From the clients I have the privilege to work with, to the projects I get to work on, I'm so blessed to be on this crazy ride. I get so many referrals now through satisfied clients. I know I'm fortunate, but I must admit, things can be crazy at times."

I was so proud of Melissa for her many successes. It was easy to see that her desire to help others and work hard was a great benefit to her business. The more she shared, the more I began to see some holes in how she managed her business growth.

"I've been so busy with the work I do I haven't taken the time to create systems for my processes. When I started all this a few years ago, it was easy to keep up with a handful of clients and the projects they hired me to complete. The way I used to structure my days hasn't changed, even though my business now has ten times as many clients as it once did."

As Melissa shared more, I learned of projects she'd delivered late to clients, invoices that were months behind, and a severe lack of personal time for her to be able to recharge her overworked battery.

Melissa was in her early thirties, and she had a fuller plate than a teenage boy at an all-you-can-eat buffet. I already confirmed that the ten-year-old Melissa I knew was still within the adult who sat across from me at the café where we met.

"You know, I work with businesses just like yours now," I mentioned. "The people I help these days aren't ten years old, but the core of what I do and how I help is quite similar to the way you first got to know me. Many of my clients run successful businesses that they've created from scratch. Can I share some tips with you?"

Melissa welcomed my tips and listened to all I had to share. In addition to tactical tips to keep up with her invoices and client projects, I also connected her with other young entrepreneurs who balanced their full profes-sional lives with active personal lives. Melissa thanked me for the connections and suggestions, and we agreed to get together again a few weeks later.

Because of her ambitious nature, I was eager to hear her updates when we met the next month. A feather could have knocked me over when Melissa told me she hadn't changed anything since we last met.

> **"A feather could have knocked me over when Melissa told me she hadn't changed anything since we last met."**

"I've been so busy," she told me. "I didn't want to connect with the people you introduced me to through email because I knew I wouldn't have the time to meet them in person. And the other ideas you shared with me? I do think I'll get to them. I just can't right now. There's so much pressure each day, and I can't let up on anything."

I called these excuses. I sensed she was attached to a different kind of checklist life than the one I'd fallen into decades before.

It turned out that Melissa—determined, warmhearted, conscientious Melissa—was fearful of the changes required to take her from a new small business owner to that of a successful leader within her company and industry.

My checklist life was filled with what I thought I was expected to do. Melissa's was full of the comfort that comes with what you know how to do. She knew how to do graphic design well. She wasn't as well-versed with business leadership, especially when that business experienced unbelievable growth.

During that second meeting, Melissa committed to learn from the mentors I connected her with, and we both committed to continue our meetings as well.

From month to month, I was thrilled to hear of Melissa's commitment to manage her business and personal growth with the guidance of her mentors. She learned from those who learned before her how to adjust her life in such a way that she could enjoy it all.

QUESTION TO CONSIDER:
Who do you admire? How can you get the most out of the lessons and knowledge they share?

ACTION TO IMPLEMENT
Find a Mentor

- Identify three to five areas of your life—personal or professional—in which you'd like to improve.
- Commit to finding a mentor who has walked the path you want to walk.
- Ask that person to mentor you, and share why you chose him/her to guide you.
- Be transparent and open-minded in your work with your mentor.

_____

_____

_____

_____

_____

_____

_____

_____

CHAPTER 13

Block the Boomerang Life

> *"Negative words are powerful boomerangs, so be careful what you say about people and yourself."*
> —MARY J. BLIGE

Think about your current life. The relationships you have. The work you do. The home you love. The stories you play on repeat in your brain.

Now think of what it would be like to be living that exact same life next year at this time. Does that thought fill your heart with joy and enthusiasm, or do you feel fear and discouragement?

If you're like most people, even people who already lead dream lives, you do want to experience continual improvement and growth. I know many people, however, who live what I call a boomerang life. A boomerang life is filled with challenges to overcome. Changes are implemented to conquer those challenges, but when they become too difficult to sustain, old habits return and the person bounces back to the original challenges.

Darlene, a former client of mine, knew all too well what it felt like to live a boomerang life. She worked in a customer call center as a supervisor and enjoyed her job, but had a greater passion for art.

"It's like a breath of the freshest spring air when I'm immersed in creative projects," she told me in her first coaching session.

She went further and shared she not only enjoyed the creation of art herself, she also reveled in opportunities to teach children to tap into their own creative senses.

Darlene reached out for coaching after learning she'd be laid off in six months. The call center would keep only a handful of current employees, and Darlene wasn't one of them.

While the layoff information shocked Darlene, she also felt a twinge of excitement. She'd lived a sheltered checklist life for four decades. It was comfortable. It was familiar. But it wasn't a life full of thrills and fun.

"It's weird," she told me during one of our sessions. "Everyone who's in the same layoff boat I'm in freaks out a little more each day, and here I am with a hint of a smile on my face. I think the layoff is a sign there's something else out there for me. The supervisory work I do is important, of course, but it's not my passion. Art, though? That's what lights me up!"

Our work included the creation of a plan for Darlene's next chapter. She wanted to paint. She wanted to teach. And she wanted to be able to do so and still pay all her bills with no problem.

The six-month window gave us time to cultivate her plan and begin implementation. I'll never forget the look on Darlene's face when she came to one of her coaching sessions. She burst through the door with a smile that lit up the room.

"Ten children signed up for my painting class! My goal is to have a max of fifteen, and I know I can fill those last five spots in the next ten days before we begin."

It was as if Darlene had started life all over again. The polite, reserved woman I'd met just a few weeks before was now a vibrant presence that everyone in her midst noticed and admired. She ignited a part of herself she'd never known before. She bid her checklist life adieu.

Darlene continued on her new life journey, and before we knew it, she had just one month of employment left at the call center. It was in that last month that I heard the whoosh of the boomerang.

While Darlene experienced success with the children she taught, she also heard comments like, "Are you sure you can do this? It's risky, you know. Not many small businesses make a go of it. You may want to find another job just to be safe. These classes are fun, but they're not a career. You need something solid, a job with benefits. You need safety."

Those words didn't come from family and friends. All that talk happened right in her own mind. Darlene's self-talk did its best to push her back to what she knew—a checklist life.

> **❝Darlene's self-talk did its best to push her back to what she knew—a checklist life.❞**

As a coach, it's not my place to tell a client what to do. My role is to listen well and help clients manage their mind so they can make the best decisions for themselves and feel confident in those decisions.

Darlene had figured out how to live her best life, and now she second-guessed herself. I wanted to push her over this obstacle of self-doubt.

Instead of telling Darlene what she should do, I asked her to catastrophize her life. "Think of the worst possible outcomes that could happen in your work as an artist and art teacher."

"What?" she asked. "That seems silly."

"Humor me," I said.

I remained patient while she made her list. She shared it with me. And then she laughed when she realized how *not* terrible those outcomes were.

In the end, Darlene rewrote those stories her brain told her. She changed her thoughts from, "What if I can't do this?" to, "Just watch me!" And the boomerang that almost reverted Darlene back to her old comfortable life whooshed right on by.

QUESTION TO CONSIDER:
How and under what circumstances has a boomerang life made an appearance in your life?

ACTION TO IMPLEMENT
Catastrophize Your Life
- As you leave your checklist life behind, list the worst outcomes that could happen as a result.
- Next to each item on your list, add an action you can take to prevent that outcome.
- In order to move forward with each action, what would you need to think and feel?

_____

_____

_____

_____

CHAPTER 14

Kick Comfort to the Curb

"Be comfortable being uncomfortable. It may get tough, but it's a small price to pay for living a dream."
—PETER MCWILLIAMS

Humans crave comfort. We like comfortable beds, comfortable shoes, comfortable recliners, even comfortable relationships. We want things to feel good, and when we find those things, it's difficult to let them go.

Have you ever worn a T-shirt well past its prime? Maybe the decal on the front was so faded you couldn't even read it anymore. It may have had holes too big to be ignored and sweat stains in the armpits. But that shirt was your friend. You loved that shirt. It was . . . comfortable. And no matter what anyone said to you, you wouldn't give it up.

Sometimes the things we find comfortable—like that ratty old T-shirt—disappear. Others in our life find ways to dispose of the things we find great comfort in, but our love for those comfort items never dies.

That mysterious disappearance can even happen in relationships that have lived past their "best by" date. The other person in the relationship, perhaps the person you thought you'd spend the rest of your life with, lets you know he/she is ready to move on, and you're not invited on the rest of the trip. Like a rug ripped out from under you, that comfort and contentment you felt in the relationship is gone, just like that T-shirt you still can't find.

Catrina's relationship with Brad had that comfy T-shirt feel to it. They met in high school, went on their first date after they graduated, and stayed together through the ups and downs of college, financial woes, career-starting jobs, friendships that formed, and friendships that faded. She was the yin to his yang, and she knew she'd be his faithful companion for life.

However, she soon learned that the comfort she enjoyed in the relationship wasn't mutual. Catrina came home from work one day and was puzzled to see boxes inside their front door. In one box she saw Brad's ratty T-shirts; in another his favorite coffee cups were stacked in a haphazard pile. The weight bench and weights he seldom used—but always said he would—were there, and even their precious cat Luna's toys, food, and bed were all piled up.

Catrina was in a fog. Her world moved in slow motion, and as the cloud lifted just a bit, she asked, "What's happening?"

Brad said, "It's time for me to leave. I'm not happy. You're not happy. It's not fair for us to live our entire lives this way."

Wait. What? Catrina didn't understand what he'd just shared. Who said they weren't happy together? And why did *he* get to decide what *they* would do?

> **"Who said they weren't happy together? And why did *he* get to decide what *they* would do?"**

How could he so nonchalantly throw away the . . . what to call it? Passion? Excitement? Adventures? No, none of those hit the mark. Finally, she found the word that escaped her. How could he throw away the *comfort* they'd had in their relationship for the past ten years?

The next few months were torturous. Catrina holed herself up in the home they'd once shared and relived every year, every month, every day of their time together. Her relationship with Brad was all she knew. He was part of her checklist life. In her mind, he was to be her husband and the father of her future children. She put all her eggs in the Brad Basket, and she couldn't see past the injustice when her checklist was ripped from her hands and her heart.

Over time and with the support of her tribe, Catrina came out of her resentment and began to see the truth she'd ignored for too long. She remembered parts of that checklist life she'd accepted even when it felt unpleasant.

"He went out a lot with his friends on Saturday nights," she told me in one of her coaching sessions. "I never told him not to go. After all, I'm not his boss or his mom. I was his girlfriend, and I didn't want to nag. I'd stay home alone and tell myself it was all okay, but every time he'd choose his friends over me, I felt unworthy, like I didn't deserve him. I wanted him to want to stay home with me, but I didn't want to force him to do so.

"Another thing I now realize—he was a job hopper, for sure. He complained about every job he had, and it's only been in these last few weeks that I've realized his constant complaints were a weight I carried for years. I paid for most of our bills and even the fun stuff we did together. Dinner out was always on me because I thought it would make him happy. All it did was drain me and my bank account and allow him to keep up with his complaints."

Today, Catrina's life looks much different than it once did. She moved to a different city where she works as marketing director of a well-known company. She spends her free time on her bike and rides for both enjoyment and competition. The more she pedals, the more she's committed to healthier food options as well.

And with each race she completes, she is gifted with a T-shirt. The kind without holes and sweat stains. The kind that represents her new, checklist-free life.

QUESTION TO CONSIDER
Where do you rely on comfort in your life? How does that comfort work against you?

ACTION TO IMPLEMENT
Move from Comfort to Discomfort

- List three areas of your life that are too comfortable and in need of revitalization.
- Develop a plan to push yourself out of your comfort zone one area at a time.
- What mindset do you need to move from your comfort zone?
- How will that mindset make you feel?
- What actions will you take to make the changes happen once you feel that way?

CHAPTER 15

_____

_____

_____

_____

_____

Rise Up with Resilience

> *"Resilience is knowing that you are the only one that has the power and the responsibility to pick yourself up."*
> —MARY HOLLOWAY

've often thought of my career as a cross-country train ride. Along the way there have been a lot of stops, and those stops allowed me to stretch my legs, explore the area, and see what's out there that I haven't yet experienced. I have friends and family members who've worked their entire career in the same industry and often the same workplace, but I've always needed that train to stop so I can recalibrate and begin a new adventure.

My train ride started with my teaching job. But after twelve years, I was restless and wanted to hop off that train. I hopped back on when I began my work at the legal services business, and the train continued on those tracks for eleven years until once again, I was ready for something new. It was time to hop off the train again and figure it out.

One train stop or career adventure began about eleven years after I started my work at the legal services business—which came twelve years after I started my teaching job. See what I mean about that cross-country trip with many stops along the way?

At that point in my career, I decided to give corporate training a shot, so I stepped on the train for this new ride. I missed my role as a teacher, and travel was of interest to me so this seemed like the perfect fit. I started a new tool-box, to which I began to add as many adult learning tools as I could. I flew all over the country each week. Most weeks I'd leave home on Sunday afternoon and come back Friday evening.

I was exhilarated by all I learned and experienced each week. I started from scratch with my own knowl-edge base and realized right away the strategies I'd used to keep kids engaged in the classroom weren't the same ones that worked with adults.

Before I realized it, my train ride career morphed into one that happened in the air. Some weeks, I'd be on six to eight flights to get to the next days' training sessions, and life felt good.

I liked the rhythm of this new career: fly, drive, teach, make a difference in the lives of professionals, and then repeat the following day. Without warning, that new life came to an abrupt halt the day I heard the diagnosis no one wants to hear.

> **ff Without warning, that new life came to an abrupt halt the day I heard the diagnosis no one wants to hear. JJ**

I sat next to my twenty-three-year-old daughter in the doctor's examination room. The room was silent as we waited for him to join us. The tests had been run, and we waited for what he was about to share with us.

We sat side by side, and I made note of how uncomfortable the chairs were. *Why would they put chairs like these in here? How many people waited in these uncomfortable chairs every day, only to be given an awful diagnosis when their butts were numb from these God-awful chairs?*

The doctor interrupted my cranky thoughts when he entered the room, looked my daughter in the eye, and said the words I dreaded. "It's cancer."

The announcement floated through the air like cotton from a cottonwood tree on a sunny spring day. The doctor left the room for a moment, and I tried to catch my breath.

After months of night sweats, shortness of breath, chest pain, and itchy skin, my daughter had done what all doctors tell us not to do: she researched her symptoms online.

When she came up with lymphoma as her ailment, I didn't believe her. The internet tells us all kinds of inaccurate information, and this couldn't be her issue. I just knew it was something else. Only it wasn't.

Don't cry, don't cry, don't cry, I told myself. *You need to be strong for her.* My heart didn't listen, though. *This is your baby. She's not supposed to be sick. This isn't fair!*

"How can you be so calm?" I asked her through tear-filled eyes.

"I'm relieved. I have a diagnosis," she said. "Now we can get to work on my treatment plan."

Her chemo treatments were scheduled every other week. Twelve treatments over six months. The new stop on my career journey didn't allow for Thursdays at home with my daughter. The other thing my new career didn't provide? Generous pay.

I hopped off the train when I was ready to quit my teaching job and do something different. I hopped back on when I went to court reporting school and worked for a business, then hopped off and on again with my new corporate training job. I can call these train stops career changes, or I can call them what they really were. They were trade-ins of one checklist for another.

I had traded in my employee checklist for an entrepreneurial one. I covered training gigs for an international training organization as an independent contractor. I was on my own when it came to benefits.

The pay for these training jobs was low, and I had accepted that part of the deal because it allowed me to fill my toolbox with new tools. The sacrifice made sense when I was able to travel every week. Not so much, though, when the doctor said those two words: "It's cancer."

Prior to that day, I felt carefree about this new career path. I jetted off here, there, and everywhere, and I loved my new work life. When I heard the doctor's words, I felt stuck. I felt hopeless. I felt sad. I felt devastated.

I told myself if I'd stayed at my last job, I'd have had benefits to allow me to care for my daughter during that difficult time. My husband and I had accumulated more savings in the past when I worked traditional jobs. We had also lived a more comfortable lifestyle than we lived at that time.

I am resilient, I told myself as I geared up to be at my daughter's chemo sessions. I was there by her side for the treatments and the after-care. I made more plain chicken wraps that year than I've ever made in my life because bland food is what she needed. I watched her young, healthy body wither away, and I hugged her gently when the pain of the drugs seemed worse than the cancer itself.

We didn't grow our savings that year, but my husband and I did learn what it meant to be frugal. We made it financially. We made it physically. We made it emotionally. And our resilience grew by leaps and bounds through it all.

QUESTION TO CONSIDER

On a scale of one to ten—with ten being most resilient—where would you rank yourself, and how can you increase that resilience score?

ACTION TO IMPLEMENT
Build Your Resilience

- Think of an area of your life that's gone in the opposite direction of how you'd like it to go.
- What action steps can you take to get that train on the track to where you want to be headed?

_____

_____

_____

_____

_____

_____

_____

_____

CHAPTER 16

Own the New You

"Life isn't about finding yourself. Life is about creating yourself."
—*GEORGE BERNARD SHAW*

One of my favorite TV shows to watch as a little girl was *The Brady Bunch*. As the seventh of eight children in my own family, I related to the Bradys' full house.

In one episode, Marcia took on a project of sorts. She brought home a girl from school—awkward, clumsy, not-at-all confident Molly. The girls' class nominated ugly duckling Molly for Senior Banquet Night host as a joke, but Marcia didn't appreciate their cruelty.

She taught Molly how to walk with confidence, how to apply makeup and style her hair, and how to answer questions with eloquence during the competition. Marcia created a new Molly who looked prettier and acted like a confident young woman. And spoiler alert: she did win the contest and invited Marcia, who came in as runner up, to co-host with her.

That new Molly is what I often think of when my coach and I discuss Future Tracy. The future version of myself doesn't experience the same challenges I do now. In fact, she's overcome those challenges and has moved on to the accomplishment of even greater feats. Future Tracy doesn't live the checklist life Past Tracy did.

And even though I'm happy to be a work in progress as I pursue the future version of myself, I sometimes feel an identity crisis may happen. Who is this Future Tracy, and is she too out of reach for me?

I'm not the only one who struggles with this future-self identity crisis. My client Ashley went from her role as an employee to that of a business owner. She is a gifted photographer who excels in everything from wedding and family photos to professional head shots and corporate videos.

Because she is an exceptional self-starter, Ashley signed her first few clients with ease and jumped into those projects. She didn't even call it work. She woke up each day eager to use her creativity to light up her clients' world.

That light shone as bright as Fourth of July fireworks for about the first six months of her new entrepreneurial journey. She was on a high each day. And then the sparks went out. It was dark. Blackout dark.

What happened? Ashley received her first taste of negative feedback from a client. His voicemail tore right through her.

> **"Ashley received her first taste of negative feedback from a client. His voicemail tore right through her."**

Ashley and I had met at a networking event a few months prior, and she'd remembered the way I described my work. I had shared that I help women clear the clutter they carry around with them, both the physical kind as well as the mental and emotional kind. She decided it was time to tackle this new challenge head on, and she hired me to coach her through it.

Her voice on our first call was shaky as she described what she'd gone through. "I was in a fetal position on my couch, and that is where I stayed. For a long, long time. I replayed that voicemail in my brain. His tone was so disrespectful, and his words stung. Why did I even decide to go into business for myself?"

Ashley went on to say that up until this negative feedback, she had celebrated the new person she was—the one who owned her own business and worked hard to sign her own clients. Even when her friends and family didn't understand her new journey, she plugged along because she knew she was a better version of herself, and she recognized how she'd thrown her checklist to the side to make way for this great dream of hers.

"I think a huge part of it is that I'm not used to this kind of feedback. At my last job, I was the one in the department who got a lot of positive recognition. I was the one asked to train new employees because I was good at what I did. At least that's how my boss described it to me. Even these last six months since I started my business, every client I've worked with has been pleased. This new feedback, though? It just spins nonstop in my brain.

"It seems ridiculous now as I share this with you, but when I was on the couch, I contemplated what to do and came up with some crazy ideas. I thought I'd reach out to my previous employer to see if they're in a position to hire me back. I also thought I may delete the voicemail and pretend I never received it."

I heard a common theme in what Ashley shared with me. It all boiled down to her desire to say goodbye to New Ashley and go back to Past Ashley. After all, our past version is easy. She's familiar to us. We're used to her. She feels comfortable.

Our brains like to sabotage our efforts as we work to be the future version of ourselves. It takes commitment and intentional effort to guide us in the direction we need to go.

As a kid, I was fascinated to see the physical changes ugly duckling Molly experienced in that half-hour *Brady Bunch* episode. What I missed at the time, and am so grateful to understand now, are the unseen, internal changes we make as we become that future version of who we are today. Those internal changes made Molly walk with confidence and joy; through her coaching journey, those same changes also helped Ashley stay out of the fetal position and move forward with strength and determination to continue on her path toward her future self.

QUESTION TO CONSIDER
What's different about the future version of yourself than the current version you are today?

ACTION TO IMPLEMENT
Create Future You
- List ten dreams you have that are so huge they seem out of reach.
- Prioritize the ten listed items with your most wanted dream at the top of your list.
- Next to each item:
  - Write a date—month, day, and year—for when it will be accomplished. Be as specific as you can.
  - Divide the overall dream into bite-size chunks.
  - Add time frames for each bite-size chunk.
  - Find an accountability partner to report your progress to.

CHAPTER 17

Forge Your New Path

> *"Do not go where the path may lead;*
> *go instead where there is no path and*
> *leave a trail."*
> —RALPH WALDO EMERSON

ions and tigers and bears. Oh my! As a child, *Wizard of Oz* night was a big deal. From the delicious smell of buttered popcorn to the sights and sounds of giggles and rambunctious kids on blankets all over the living room floor, Dorothy and her friends created great excitement for us. This, of course, was in the years before VCRs and DVDs and streaming movies, so the Wizard wasn't available to us at the press of a button. We waited with anticipation each year for this special experience.

It was Dorothy's path, that yellow brick road, that always mesmerized me. Her world filled with color the moment she entered the Land of Oz. It's only now that I realize those yellow bricks were Dorothy's checklist. She needed to follow the path just as she'd been told to get to Emerald City so the Wizard could get her back home—and provide one friend a brain, another a heart, and yet another great courage.

She followed that path like I'd followed my checklist life for so many years. There were obstacles in the way for both Dorothy and me, but we didn't give up. Dorothy continued along those sunshiny bricks, and I pushed myself to achieve more, be more, do more, and add as many checks to my checklist as possible.

My client Renee was on her own yellow brick road when we began our work together. She was employed by the same organization for seventeen years and told me her job was fine. Now for some people, fine is a positive descriptor. For Renee, I sensed her "fine" answer was a veil she'd placed over her head to protect herself from others' reactions to her perspective about that job. I sensed her desire for a world she couldn't yet describe but still very much wanted.

Renee and I clicked right away, and if it were possible to have met Dorothy in real life, she'd have been one of us, too. We were the Conformist Clique. All rule followers. All checklist keepers. We lived life on the safe side. Lives we liked to call fine.

"In all honesty, there's nothing wrong with my job," she told me. "I've earned promotions over the years, and I believe in the company's mission. I've gotten to the point, though, where I believe that although there's nothing wrong with it, there's not a lot that excites me about it. It's all fine. It's just not incredible."

Her job and the fine-ness of it was no different than Dorothy's realization that her meticulous trip on that yellow brick road only brought her to a little man behind a curtain who pretended to be something he wasn't. Renee knew it was time for a change. Her checklist life had gotten her to fine, but she wanted sensational. The scary part? She didn't have a nice little detour off the yellow brick road to follow. She needed to forge a brand-new path.

> **❝The scary part? She didn't have a nice little detour off the yellow brick road to follow.❞**

It's ironic that my fabulous childhood memory of the wonderful *Wizard of Oz* had become a metaphor for what held me back in life. Even more ironic is the lesson at the end of that story when Dorothy and her peeps all find that the things they wanted were available to them all along. The trip back home was as easy as three clicks of the heels, and the desired brain, heart, and courage were always at the characters' disposal.

The same was true for Renee. She was at first apprehensive about her new path, but with some encouragement, she began her search for a new job.

She updated her resume and LinkedIn profile, and shared on one of our coaching calls, "I devote a block of time every day to my job search and have shared my goal with some close friends and business acquaintances. It feels good to unlock this part of me. I'd gotten so stagnant with what I did, and I thought I just needed to accept that that's how it had to be as I moved through my career. Now I realize it's all in my control. I know I will find the perfect job for me."

As her search continued, so did her anticipation. She felt she'd unlocked a part of herself she hadn't even realized had been sealed tight for years. Her excitement grew each day as she learned of the opportunities available to her.

Six weeks into her job search, with a bit of trepidation to go along with a new sense of adventure, Renee accepted a job offer. She would start that new job in a different industry where she'd earn a higher salary and the opportunity to apply the leadership skills she'd sharpened over the past several years.

It's strange to think that just a few weeks prior, Renee couldn't even put into words what she wanted in her professional life. She'd thought everything was fine. She had filled out her checklist and followed all the rules she'd created for herself.

"I gave my notice today," she told me on one of our calls. "I'll be here for another month, and then I start my new job. One more month at this place I've been at for seventeen years. Wow! This feels surreal."

During her last month, Renee trained her replacement, solidified her documentation of processes and procedures, and received more positive feedback than she'd heard in the past decade and a half.

QUESTION TO CONSIDER
In what part of your life do you want to grow from fine to fabulous?

ACTION TO IMPLEMENT
Pave Your Own Yellow Brick Path
- Choose one area of your life where you'd like to go off course.
- Draw a path on paper and mark where you are now at the start of the path.
- Add your final destination.
- Step into your creativity to add stops along the way to get you from where you are to where you want to be.

_____

_____

_____

CHAPTER 18

Find Some New Firsts

"Firsts are best because they are beginnings."

—JENNY HAN,

P.S. I Still Love You (To All the Boys I've Loved Before)

The day after I got married, I wrote a paper for school. The paper was due on Monday, and I had yet to begin on Sunday afternoon.

My college years were long enough ago that I didn't use a computer; instead, I used a clunky typewriter with the inevitable correction tape at the ready.

Clunk, clunk, clunk went the rhythm of my fingers on the machine while my brain did its best to care about the topic of the paper I wrote. As my brain and fingers continued their cadence, my peripheral vision registered the person who stood next to me. My new husband.

"What should we have for dinner?" he asked. Oh, wow. This was new. I wasn't used to this.

My first answer wasn't great. "No idea," I said as my fingers continued their dance on the keys.

All I knew was that I had about fourteen hours until this paper was due, and at this rate, I was afraid I might still be typing away at that time.

I tried to figure out what we could muster up with the items in our bare fridge and cabinets when he said, "Let's have fried chicken!"

"Ummm . . . I've never made fried chicken," I replied. I'd grown up with a mom who did everything for everyone, and I now realized she'd done it all quite well. Perhaps too well.

"Don't worry," new hubby said. "I've got this!"

I stayed at the kitchen table and pounded away on the keyboard while he cracked the eggs, poured flour on a plate, and began the messy dipping job needed for the tastiest fried chicken.

With each step, he asked me if he'd done it right. I wasn't sure. The only thing I did know for sure was that we couldn't eat chicken that wasn't all the way done or we'd both end up in the hospital, and we didn't have the money for that.

After a while, the crispy chicken came out of the pan at the same time I put the final touches on my paper. We each put a piece of chicken on our plates, looked at each other, took a bite, and smiled.

"We did it!" he said. "It tastes so good! We do know how to make fried chicken!" I cherished his obvious generosity in his pronoun use, for *we* hadn't done any such thing, but even now, more than three decades into our marriage, we bring up that first meal together.

Some firsts are like that. They warm our hearts and help us remember the beginning of a journey in our life. Whether it be a marriage, a job, a new skill, or the many firsts we experience as parents, our first shot at something can feel amazing.

And then there are the other firsts, the ones that don't always start so well. Shelley came to me as she worked through one of those firsts. She was in her early fifties and shared that she'd worked various jobs through most of her married life. She did so to help pay the bills as she and her husband raised their three children, but in all those years she'd never been passionate about any job she'd had. That is, until she started her current job.

Her career had taken a turn for the better six months prior when she was promoted to a leadership position. She accepted the additional pay, additional responsibilities, and, as it turned out, additional hours required to get it all done.

By now her kids were grown and out of the house, and she thrived in her new role. "I enjoy it all so much," she told me. "I guide and mentor my team, which I love. I've also learned how to get underperforming team members to step it up and become valuable members of the team. My boss has recognized me more than once for what she calls the miracles I've created."

Shelley rode the wave and flourished in her job for the first time in her career, but this first didn't make everyone as happy as it did Shelley. Her husband wasn't used to this. Her long hours at the office and the work travel she'd begun didn't sit well with him. He was used to a different arrangement, and rather than adjust to her incredible first, he reacted in a negative way.

> **"Shelley rode the wave and flourished in her job for the first time in her career, but this first didn't make everyone as happy as it did Shelley."**

"This is ridiculous," he told her one night after her thirteen-hour work day. "You can't keep up like this, and I won't have it. It's time to look for another job, one that pays you for a normal eight-hour work day and doesn't expect you to give them more time than you give your own husband!"

"How can he be so cruel when I feel I've found my calling?" Shelley asked me. "I spent all those years in jobs to help support our family, and I didn't do that just for financial reasons. It was also for emotional reasons. I was there for anything our kids needed. Now it's my turn!"

Shelley spoke of divorce as her anguish grew, but in the end, it was simple boundary setting that turned things around for her husband and her. They were open and honest with each other when they communicated about the changes they'd experienced as a result of her new job.

"He even told me that he's noticed I seem happier and am more confident. He said he's so proud of me and didn't want anyone to take advantage of me and the time I put into the job. When I explained that I feel the work I do is a privilege, not a chore, he nodded and told me he'll always be my biggest fan. That melted my heart."

For Shelley and her husband, there were some new firsts. Date nights, last-minute getaways, and sci-fi movie marathons on the weekends. The onetime checklist life where she worked to bring home a paycheck was long gone, and for the two of them, they couldn't have been happier to toss that checklist aside.

QUESTION TO CONSIDER

What new firsts are you experiencing in your life right now? If your answer is none, what new firsts would you like to have?

ACTION TO IMPLEMENT
Ride the New Firsts Train

- Choose one thing you'd like to do for the first time.
- Map out a plan for how you can make that first happen.
  - What do you need to learn before you can begin?
  - How can you block the time for it?
  - Who will you need help from?
  - What time frame do you give yourself to complete your new first?
- Then go to work to implement your plan!

_____

_____

_____

_____

_____

_____

CHAPTER 19

Make the Proof Go Poof

"The only validation we need comes from within; whatever our souls allow is allowed."
—SHERIHAN GAMAL

A tool I like to use in my business is the DISC assessment. Many people call the DISC a personality test; I prefer behavioral inventory. The DISC shows people how they choose to use certain behaviors that are part of who they are. Once they understand where they are on the DISC scale, they are able to better understand their behavior toward others and how to best tailor that behavior in different circumstances.

For those unfamiliar with the DISC, each letter represents a different type of behavior, and people who take the assessment are able to see where they score for each of the four pillars: D (Decisive/Dominance), I (Interactive/Influence), S (Stabilizing/Steadiness), and C (Cautious/ Conscientious). I score quite high in the C pillar, which means I'm a rule follower. I dot my i's and cross my t's; I don't miss deadlines; I like facts, figures, research, and proof.

That high C has both helped and hindered me in life. I am the person who doesn't need help to stick with my schedule. When I tell a client I'll call at 3:00, she knows it won't be a minute after. My husband even comments about how lucky he is to have married me—let's just bask in that fabulous compliment for a moment—because he's never had to worry about late fees on our bills. I've got them all scheduled to arrive on time—not too early, not ever late, but just right. I'm the Goldilocks of the plan, the schedule, the menu, the rules.

> **❝I'm the Goldilocks of the plan, the schedule, the menu, the rules.❞**

And that last comment is where my hindrance begins. Remember that pregnancy at the age of eighteen? Well, let's just say the high C inside me threw a huge temper tantrum when I broke the rule of college first, then marriage and kids. That was how the checklist was supposed to look in the eyes of my high C. My brain tells me I have to do it right. No room for mistakes. Lots of boxes to check. And to keep up with this part of who I am, I have often relied on proof or evidence that I show up in the best possible light in all instances.

The proof I've needed in life has shown up in many ways. I have two college diplomas that fill up my high C bucket. They're the validation I've always felt I needed to prove to myself—and others—that I do things right. I didn't finish a doctoral program. After the first thirty-two hours were earned, I learned I'd need to travel a couple of times each week to complete the program. I didn't move forward with that plan and used the reason—excuse— that my kids and husband needed me at home.

It seemed too big of a mountain to climb and was one of the first times in life I felt I gave up. And I'm not a person who gives up. I do everything right, right? I check off those boxes with the best of them.

I heard from coworkers for years that I'm an excep- tional listener. I always appreciated this feedback, but that's as far as it went. A few years ago, I tuned in to the fact that when I provided corporate training sessions throughout the country, people came up to me during breaks to ask questions about what we'd just discussed. They'd say, "I didn't want to bring this up in front of the group, but I have this issue with a coworker. Here's what happened. What should I do?" I realized I coached people during my breaks, which prompted me to obtain my coach's certification.

I researched programs, and my high C told me what I needed to do. I needed one of those certification programs that cost as much as my doctoral degree would have. I needed the validation of another piece of paper to provide proof that I had done things right. I needed the endorsement of the world for my accomplishments. And then I read the quote shared at the beginning of this chapter:

"The only validation we need comes from within; whatever our souls allow is allowed."

And I made a decision. It was a decision my high C has gotten over, but we weren't on speaking terms for a while. I signed up for a smaller, shorter, less expensive coaching program, and I did something quite extraordinary. I built a successful coaching business because I now know that my validation doesn't come from external checklists. It has come from within me all along.

QUESTION TO CONSIDER
What perceived proof or need for validation is holding you back from living your best life?

ACTION TO IMPLEMENT
Create Your Best Life Without Proof

- Think back over your life and focus on an experience when you felt you needed validation from other people or circumstances.
- How did it feel to need that validation?
- Rewrite that story of the past. How would it feel for you to relive that experience without the need for validation?
- Now take that newfound freedom from validation and set a goal for yourself, one you can accomplish because you want to and not because you need any proof of the grestness within you.

_____

_____

_____

_____

_____

_____

CHAPTER 20

Take Responsibility

*"It's only when you take responsibility for
your life that you discover
how powerful you truly are."*
—ALLANAH HUNT

You've heard of Negative Nelly, right? How about Blameless Bob? Rumor has it they live together in a house full of miserable conversations that sound like this:

"Nothing ever goes right for me!"

"Well, don't blame me; it's not my fault!"

All kidding aside, I'd venture to say we all know people who stay stuck in the glass-half-empty mindset. After a while, we numb ourselves to the negativity and often jump on the bandwagon and scan for all that's wrong with the world. For many it's easier and more familiar to do this than it is to look for positivity.

Negativity has always been one of my triggers—and, yes, I've fallen into the pit at times myself—but the blame versus responsibility theme is something I haven't always tuned in to.

I explain it to clients this way: Picture a horizontal line. Blame is at one end of the line, and responsibility is at the other. Now take that horizontal line and lift the responsibility end of it. If we added a marble to the responsibility side, it would roll down the line to the blame side. Science tells us this is due to gravity. Another way to look at it, though, is that it's so much easier to move to blame than it is to accept responsibility for circumstances we encounter.

> **"Picture a horizontal line. Blame is at one end of the line, and responsibility is at the other."**

Such was the case for Linda when she hired me to help her build her new business. She had achieved modest success but knew she was capable of more. We began our weekly coaching sessions, and it became immediately clear that she spent a great deal of time on the blame end of the line. It seemed it was always someone else's fault.

She explained things away with, "The client called and complained because his invoice was screwed up. I swear my employees never get anything right!" and, "I couldn't believe it when my friend Nancy got out of her car at my house and slipped and fell on the driveway. My husband knew there was ice out there. Why in the world wouldn't he have put some ice melt down?" and even, "I rushed into the meeting with my new client late yesterday. I hate to give that kind of first impression. I told him it wasn't my fault. The lady in front of me at the coffee shop had the longest coffee order ever. I have no idea how the barista could have gotten it right. Talk about a custom order!"

The overarching theme in all I heard from Linda? *Not my fault!*

It was far too easy for me to relate to Linda's Blame Game world because I used to be a resident myself. I navigated my life with my checklist as my personal GPS, and I learned when I encountered failure, either I ended up in the hot seat or someone else did. The more practice I got, the more natural it became to give someone else that honor.

When my job as a teacher didn't work out for me, I blamed the administration. They didn't understand what it was like to teach thirty-plus kids who spanned three to five different grade and ability levels. They weren't the ones in the classroom who tried to do it right every day. In court reporting school, I'd look at the young women fresh out of high school and think about how easy they had it. They didn't have to juggle a full-time job, three kids, a husband, and a long commute, which must mean they had all the time they needed to practice moving their fingers as fast as they could on that little machine. Another great Blame Game story I'd tell myself was that I didn't have any sort of management education so I couldn't be expected to lead as well as those who did.

It takes twenty-one days of consistent behavior to develop a habit. Once we've developed it, it's automatic. The same is true for the Blame Game. The more we blame others for what doesn't go well, the more reflexive it becomes to continue doing so.

I worked hard to exit the Blame Game world and instead take responsibility for every result I have in life. It's one of the best lessons I've ever learned, and one I'm able to share with my clients.

When we blame others, we protect ourselves from the failures that are an inevitable part of life. For me, I'd always had my checklist to push me in one direction or the other. When I hit a brick wall of failure, I'd look to my external world for that failure's source rather than look in the mirror so I could work to improve my results. My client Linda followed that same pattern.

One day I asked Linda to share with me how her last week had gone. As she talked, I wrote down every name she mentioned. After about ten minutes of the debrief of her week, I showed her my list. She looked at the names of her husband, her sister, three friends, the FedEx delivery man, two clients, and a nameless convenience store clerk. Her face went blank when I asked, "What do all of these people have in common?"

"They've all been part of my life this past week?" she asked.

"What else?" I pushed.

"Ummm . . . "

I then asked, "Who is responsible for the success of your company? Who is solely, unequivocally, full-steam-ahead responsible?"

"Me?" she hesitantly answered.

"What?" I asked, hand cupped to my ear.

"Me!" she shouted.

"Then don't give others your power. Take responsibility. Leave blame in your bottom drawer under all those shirts you no longer wear, and don't pick it back up again."

This was the turning point in Linda's coaching and also in her business. Blame is easy. It's the path of least resistance at the bottom end of that horizontal line, but responsibility—for our successes and our failures—is where we find the answers to everything we need in life.

QUESTION TO CONSIDER
In which areas of your life do you focus on blame rather than responsibility?

ACTION TO IMPLEMENT
Grab Responsibility by the Horns

- At the top of a piece of paper, write an area of your life where you go into blame mode.
- Answer the following questions:
  - What thoughts do I have that make me go into blame mode?
  - How does it feel once I'm there?
  - What viable solutions arrive when I'm in blame mode?
  - How might my solutions be different if I moved to responsibility mode?

_____

_____

_____

_____

_____

_____

CHAPTER 21

Travel Your New Path

> *"I see my path, but I don't know where it leads. Not knowing where I'm going is what inspires me to travel it."*
> —ROSALIA DE CASTRO

Every year in May and June I get a bit sappy when I hear the inspirational commencement speeches given at graduations. I think back to when I graduated from high school and college and realize I didn't comprehend at that time what a blank slate my life was.

I had the opportunity—the privilege—to be whoever I wanted to be and go after whatever goals I set for myself. I had the ability to create my own path in life. I still see that as a privilege, but I also see it as an immense responsibility. How was I to know in my twenties who I wanted to be and how I wanted to show up in the world?

It was so much easier to glance at the checklist and follow the steps I'd created through my observations over the years.

My marriage was one of the first checkmarks in my adult life, something my client Theresa and I had in common. She, too, married young, at the age of twenty-one, and for the most part followed a predictable checklist life. She had her daughter at twenty-three. She and her husband were high school sweethearts, and when she looked at him, even twenty years later, she saw a world of great possibility in his eyes. He was her protector, her sidekick, her cheerleader, her one true love. Until he wasn't.

For a long time, Theresa didn't tune in to the small changes in her husband. He arrived home late from work more often than usual, he could barely get up in the mornings, and he asked her if he could take some cash from her wallet a few times a week.

None of these individual changes seemed like anything to be suspicious about, but when she looked in her wallet on a random Tuesday and saw it had been picked clean—no bills, no change, and one credit card gone—she knew something wasn't right.

Theresa called her husband's cell phone. "Hey, I'm on my way to the dry cleaners and see that I don't have any cash and my credit card is gone. Do you have my card and cash?" As she said the words, she laughed nervously.

"Uh, yeah," he answered. "I thought I told you I needed the cash to pick something up today. I just took the credit card in case the cash wasn't enough. Thought I told you. Sorry about that. Be home soon."

He didn't arrive home soon. He didn't arrive home that night at all. Theresa called him, left voicemails, sent texts, and when his voicemail was full, she called over and over again. She was alone and worried, and she was more scared than she'd ever been.

This led Theresa to investigate. "I started to see the proof of his drug addiction when I took the time to put all the little things together from the past few months. I was in shock when I figured it out," she shared in one of our coaching sessions.

How could he have done this right under her nose? How could it have gone on for almost a year without her knowledge? And how could he have cleaned out their emergency fund she now wanted to use to send him to rehab?

> **❝How could he have done this right under her nose? How could it have gone on for almost a year without her knowledge?❞**

This wasn't the path Theresa ever thought she'd travel on, but she knew she'd vowed to stay by her husband in good times and in bad. She worked hard to find the funds needed for his rehab, and family members supported her with this as well as the emotional scars she'd acquired from the lies he'd told to keep his habit a secret.

When her husband left for rehab, Theresa knew she needed to fill her life with something other than the pain, fear, and anger that had become all too familiar. She began to work on her own personal development. She joined a support group for family members of addicts, began attending church again, read personal development books, and went on long walks with her cherished black lab, Bruce.

"This isn't the life I imagined I'd have," she told me, "but I know I can't give up on myself. At first I wanted to drop everything on my own plate so I could devote all my time to him and his recovery, but I realized if I did that, I'd lose myself."

Theresa had hit a crossroads in her life. The path she'd created for herself many years ago was now rocky and rough and not a path she enjoyed at all. She created her new path and became a better version of herself. Her checklist was thrown away with each step she took to ease the pain of her husband's betrayal.

Theresa's husband returned home from rehab and did his best to live a clean life. He still struggles and has been in rehab again but doesn't give up on his goal to kick his addiction for good. And Theresa, because of her commitment to herself, doesn't fall apart when her husband relapses. She's strong, she's determined, and she's committed to the love she has for her new path.

QUESTION TO CONSIDER

How do you travel, or prepare to travel, a new path in life? How does that travel improve your life?

ACTION TO IMPLEMENT
Lace Up Your Shoes for the Journey

- Your new path requires you to do things differently than you've done them before. Consider the following:
  - ° What emotions arise as you begin to think about the new path you'll travel?
  - ° How can you move from negative emotions to positive ones so you'll have the fuel you'll need?
  - ° Who will ride shotgun with you on your new path?
  - ° When does your journey begin?
- When we travel a new path, it isn't easy, but it is possible. Now that you've answered the questions above, create your step-by-step plan, and take your first step on that new path.

CHAPTER 22

_____

_____

_____

_____

Dive into Uncharted Territory

*"Life is uncharted territory. It reveals its story
one moment at a time."*
—LEO BUSCAGLIA

It was **Monday morning.** The world was up; coffee flowed from favorite insulated cups and highways were packed solid with people ready to begin their work week.

I was at home, and I remember my husband's efforts to be supportive of his train-wreck wife. "Just take it easy today. Relax. You deserve that."

I didn't have a job to go to on that particular Monday. I'd quit mine when the frustration and overwhelm of my job became too much for me.

After I submitted my resignation at the legal services business, I stayed an additional month to wrap things up. I felt empowered during that month about my plan to start a new, unknown career path that would allow me to do something better suited to my strengths. That empowerment wasn't with me in the kitchen that Monday morning, though.

My husband walked out the door with his own coffee, and within seconds the drama that swirled in my brain flowed through my arms and came out my fingertips onto the keyboard. Where should I begin? What should I do with my life? The vast possibilities excited me and made me queasy at the same time. Relax today? I don't think so, dear hubby.

"Where should I begin? What should I do with my life? The vast possibilities excited me and made me queasy at the same time."

After some soul searching—that took quite a bit longer than that one Monday—I decided to work as a certified corporate trainer. I'd taught kids at one point in my career and thought training adults would allow me to use the strengths that once helped me in the classroom.

I remember a feeling of exhilaration when I was gone from home for the week-long certification process, and I was inspired when I met others in my group who had come from all walks of life. Within a few weeks I was on the road every week, and I traveled by plane, rental car, and Uber.

I built a very different life for myself, and that internal battle between excitement and queasiness continued. I was in uncharted territory. Sometimes I was partnered with other, more experienced trainers, and I'd watch in awe as they reached into their figurative bags of tricks to engage adults in the content they shared. I had the bag, but it was empty.

As with anything in life, the more training work I did, the better I got. The more I fell flat on my face with some groups, the more I learned what not to do the next time.

A couple years after my venture into corporate training, I saw a LinkedIn post from Lee, a man who'd been in my training certification class with me. I reached out to him, and we agreed to catch up by phone a few days later.

I learned that Lee no longer provided the type of corporate training we'd both been certified to deliver. He now coached executives and worked on an ongoing basis helping various organizations improve their overall results. He shared that he always started clients with a behavioral assessment and asked if I'd like to take it. "Sure!" I replied. "I love that kind of stuff."

A few days later we reviewed my results by phone while I sat in a coffee shop with the results pulled up on my laptop. Lee verified some information I already knew about myself. I like things to be structured rather than off the cuff. I have a strength in developing others. Patience comes easily for me. Self-esteem is not a strong attribute of mine. *Wait. What?*

But that wasn't all. Self-assessment, self-confidence, and self-management all showed up at the low end of my scores. As Lee continued to explain my results, I began to choke up. I looked up from my computer screen to find an elderly man at a table about six feet away, holding a book without reading it. He looked over the top of his reading glasses at me, the strange woman in the coffee shop with tears flowing down her cheeks.

I wiped the tears away and told myself to stop. I needed to hear this information. Lee asked, "When you finish a training session with a group, and some of them come up to you afterward to tell you how much they enjoyed it, how does that make you feel?"

"Incredible," I replied. "Like I made the right decision to get into this field."

"And then when you hop in the car to head home and you berate yourself because you skipped something you'd planned to say or messed up a quote you shared . . . "

How in the world did Lee know that even when I got praise from training groups, I still beat myself up on the way home? He wasn't at those training sessions with me, and I knew he didn't live in my brain. I felt like I was on *Candid Camera.*

Lee could see in my assessment results that I excelled from an external standpoint. The outside world saw Tracy perform well. Inside, I questioned my every move, every word, every mistake. It was normal to beat myself up.

And then Lee said, "You can make the decision to stay the same as you are now, or you can make changes to have the business and life of your dreams. Which is it?"

No surprise here. I said yes to Lee and his coaching program. I said yes to the positive changes I needed to make to become the best version of myself. And I said yes to the uncharted territories ahead of me.

QUESTION TO CONSIDER
What uncharted territory have you shied away from? How could it help you on your journey to your best future self?

ACTION TO IMPLEMENT
Get Your Diving Gear On

Divide a piece of paper into four quadrants by drawing one vertical line down the center from top to bottom and one horizontal line across the center from left to right.

- In quadrant one, write one uncharted territory you'd like to explore in your life.
- In quadrant two, write why that uncharted territory is something you want.
- In quadrant three, write how you can make it happen.
- In quadrant four, write when you'd like to be able to dismiss the uncharted part of the description. In other words, you will have done it by that date.

_____

_____

_____

_____

_____

CHAPTER 23

Talk to Your Truth Tellers

"Tell your story. Shout it. Write it. Whisper it if you have to. But tell it. Some won't understand it. Some will outright reject it. But many will thank you for it. And then the most magical thing will happen. One by one, voices will start whispering, 'Me, too.' And your tribe will gather. And you will never feel alone again."
—L. R. KNOST

enna and I connected the moment we met. Have you ever experienced that? You meet someone, and within minutes you feel as if you've known the person for years. She spoke my language, understood what I meant when my words didn't provide great clarity, and made me feel comfortable and included right from the start. It reminded me of how I feel when I wear my favorite, fluffy pink robe, the one I wear so often my husband calls me Pinky. It just felt . . . right.

Jenna was on the leadership team for one of my first business clients where I provided team development services. Those services included leadership development, conflict resolution, time management, and customer service. I help with what many call "people stuff." I often say I provide drama detox.

At the core of what I do for organizations like Jenna's is help every employee understand that what he/she does brings great value. They have worth. They are important. And the world is a better place because of them.

It's perhaps no surprise that the talk of value and worth is not how I promote my team development services. The leaders who hire me want the work to get done faster and better with few to no mistakes. I don't talk about value and worth. I talk about increased productivity, improved conflict management, and enhanced customer service.

My heart is there for the foundational effects of value and worth, not just the end results of those two aspects. I believe with every ounce of my being that when people feel valued and worthy, they show up with more confidence, engagement, and contentment in whatever it is they do. They are better parents, spouses, siblings, friends, leaders, and employees when their insides light up with self-love and respect.

> **❝I believe with every ounce of my being that when people feel valued and worthy, they show up with more confidence, engagement, and contentment in whatever it is they do.❞**

The day I met with the decision makers at Jenna's company, we discussed a lack of productivity and an abundance of inter-office conflict and customer service issues. As I shared how I could help, I saw a glint in Jenna's eyes that told me she understood there was something more to what I provide. I was hired that day and began my work with their teams.

Jenna had a welcoming vibe right from the start, and I enjoyed my time with her. As I got to know her better, I learned she also carried a lot of weight on her shoulders. She managed a great deal in the office, and while she often seemed to do it with ease, I noticed a change in her over the course of several months. Her boss demanded a lot from her and had little empathy for all Jenna juggled. She called on Jenna often and expected her to drop whatever was on her plate so she could take care of her boss's needs, regardless of the time of day or night. I noticed more weariness in Jenna the longer I was there.

In addition to the work I did with their team as a whole, Jenna and I also took time each month for leadership coaching. Jenna soaked up our discussions like a sponge and was always eager to learn new tactics to help her improve in her role. One day, the weight on her shoulders seemed to drag her all the way down, and I mentioned what I observed. It was as if a dam broke when Jenna's tears began to flow.

"This is not my best life," she said, "and the stress of my work life now spills over into my personal life. I lose patience so fast with my kids and husband, and my time with friends is non-existent. I'm at the point where I dread the thought of being here each day."

That feeling of worth and value I aspire to ignite in everyone I work with was nonexistent for Jenna. She spun her wheels and gave her all, but felt she did it all for naught.

As our conversation continued, I learned Jenna carried a large dose of guilt with her each day. She felt guilty for all she put into her job at her family's expense. She felt guilty she never got back to friends when they'd reach out. She felt guilty when she was annoyed and angry at her boss. And she felt guilty when she thought about the disappointment her coworkers may feel if she left the company.

Jenna and I had moved from a strong initial connection to a relationship of truth tellers. Jenna's truth was that she longed to be respected for the work she did. She longed for boundaries between her work life and her home life. She longed to let go of the guilt that plagued her. And she longed for a life that felt easier and more enjoyable. I assured Jenna that she deserved everything she longed for.

We got to work on a plan for a discussion between Jenna and her boss so she could share her truth. As we prepared the plan, she decided she would resign from the company. When she carried out the plan and talked with her boss, she made the decision to stay. It wasn't a raise or better bonus structure that changed her decision. It wasn't the intense feeling of guilt of letting others down, either.

It was a realization that filled her up from the inside out: she did bring value, she did have inherent worth, and she was a strong leader eager to tackle the obstacles in her path with the open, honest truth.

QUESTION TO CONSIDER
How and why do you hide your truth? When you choose to share it, how could it open up your world to greater possibilities?

ACTION TO IMPLEMENT
Speak Your Truth
- Write three lies you tell yourself or others.
- Under each lie, write what you lose when you don't tell the truth.
- Under each loss, write what you could gain when you change those lies to truths.
- Determine if the changes from lie to truth will happen within you or if conversations with others are needed.
- If conversations are necessary, schedule them in the next month.
- Follow through on those conversations.
- Live your truth, and enjoy the rewards you reap!

CHAPTER 24

Unlock the Cuffs

"When facts give way to faith, then and only then do you unlock the possibilities within."
—TEMITOPE IBRAHIM

don't think I know anyone who's been handcuffed and taken away to jail, but I do believe that I was the recipient of golden handcuffs for many years of my career. Benefits like health insurance and retirement plans—along with the obvious paycheck—helped me feel safe in my jobs, but kept me locked in those shiny cuffs. With the cuffs on my wrists, I was well able to check off the boxes on my checklist. I did things the way I was supposed to do them according to my parents, society, and, of course, the checklist.

I've learned from my own coaches that familiar pain is often chosen over unfamiliar pain, and that's the premise I followed. Some coworkers were difficult to deal with, but I came to expect the bad behavior they brought with them each day, and I did little to try to improve the situation. Some policies didn't work well for me, but it was all part of the deal. Even in personal relationships, I would settle for what another person said and did rather than speak up when those words and actions didn't sit well with me. The pain I felt in many situations nagged at me, but it was familiar. I knew what to expect, and for some odd reason, I decided it was nicer to know that than it would be to venture out to new jobs and relationships where I'd risk different, unfamiliar pain.

My friend Libby got a taste of unfamiliar pain when her boss of a dozen years retired, and another leader took over as CEO. Libby was revered by her former boss and had free rein in her role with the organization. This was not the case with her new boss, which made Libby feel like she'd been imprisoned in a different type of handcuffs.

I was used to Libby's spirited nature and noticed a change in her one evening over dinner. "Are you okay?" I asked. "You don't seem like yourself tonight."

"I think I'm dying," she said, "but it's not a quick death. It's slow and painful and irritating as all get out."

Did I mention Libby had a splash of drama in her as well?

As I asked for more details, Libby shared, "My new boss—it's all her fault. She accepts none of my ideas, and you know how creative I am. It's like she doesn't even listen before her head shakes no. I've been stifled. I feel stuck. And, oh yeah, I'm dying. Did I mention that already?"

When situations like this pop up, I like to ask if I should wear my friend hat or my coach hat. "Oh, I need the coaching. Put on that hat, and coach away," she told me.

I learned the new CEO did not have a background in healthcare, although Libby's organization was in the healthcare industry. Libby saw great importance in compassion, empathy, and understanding. Part of her job was to go out in the community and educate people on all her organization could do to help those in need. Her new CEO wanted facts, figures, and as much data as she could get her hands on. Libby's prior methods to spread the word about her organization's services were in direct opposition to the CEO's craving for numbers.

Libby felt cemented in place, and the cuffs couldn't have been any tighter on her wrists. She was so worked up she thought she might quit on the spot the next day. To Libby, this unfamiliar pain was too much to bear. She wanted things to go back to the way they used to be even though, after much discussion, I learned everything wasn't perfect with her last boss.

"Libby felt cemented in place, and the cuffs couldn't have been any tighter on her wrists."

It was true Libby was able to make some decisions on her own, but her old boss didn't always follow through with her end of the deal. That, for Libby, was familiar pain. The cuffs were on, but Libby was used to the type of pain those cuffs caused. These new cuffs caused blisters for Libby.

She agreed that evening that she wouldn't quit her job the next day or for the next six months. She committed to half a year to learn more about her new boss, understand how to communicate better with her, and continue to give her all every day. Four months into that six-month commitment, Libby and I were at dinner again, and she shared how much she'd gained because of the commitment she kept. Her handcuffs were unlocked, and she felt like an even more competent and integral member of the team.

As for my experience with handcuffs, I don't believe it was others who put them on me. I put them on myself and settled into a life of box checking as I lowered my expectations. When I learned how to unlock the cuffs on my own, my world opened up to new and better opportunities; just like Libby, my new life without blisters on my wrists felt better than anything I could have imagined.

QUESTION TO CONSIDER
Where and when do you wear handcuffs that keep you in a familiar pain cycle?

ACTION TO IMPLEMENT
Find the Key to Your Cuffs

- Think of three circumstances that prompt negative reactions from you.
- When you think about one of those circumstances, what physical symptoms pop up? For example:
  - Does your heart beat faster?
  - Are you short of breath?
  - Does color rise up your neck and over your face?
- Now think about what it would take to change those negative reactions to responses that serve you better. For example:
  - What if you make your coworker's criticism mean nothing about you?
  - What if you showcased your talents at a job where you felt excited and empowered every day?
  - What if the way your partner looks at you makes you feel more loved and more loving?
- What physical symptoms do you have as a result of the new thoughts you have?
- How can your improved physical symptoms and thoughts help you unlock your current cuffs?

CHAPTER 25

Ditch the Excuses

"Hold yourself responsible for a higher standard than anyone else expects of you. Never excuse yourself."
—HENRY WARD BEECHER

"**I don't have enough** time/money."
"I'm too young/old/fat/thin/tired/experienced/inexperienced."
"I don't have the right connections."
"My parents/family/friends don't believe I can."

All classic excuses. Excuses for why people aren't where they want to be in life. Excuses for why people don't try something new. Excuses to fail ahead of time. Why try and risk failure when we can just fail in advance, right?

I was once the Empress of Excuses. I told myself I couldn't accomplish whatever it was that seemed out of reach for me because I married young/had kids to raise/didn't have time for one more thing/earned a paltry teacher's salary/didn't have the support of family/lacked the degree or certification needed. Did you notice many of those excuses were also the line items on my checklist? That made it nice and easy to hang back, complain, and not accomplish what I wanted to accomplish in life.

I had traded in my empress crown by the time I met Becky at a networking event. She was impressive and stood out for all the right reasons. She had fiery red hair and wore huge costume jewelry and tall, patent leather boots with horses all over them. She didn't blend into the background, that was for sure, and when she spoke, she made people want to hear more.

As with most networking events I attend, each of us was invited to give a thirty-second elevator speech of who we are and how we help.

"Hi, I'm Becky, and I'm da bomb when it comes to being a mom, wife, daughter, sister, and friend. I tossed out my employee cap a few years ago so I could spend more time with my family. Now I get to wear boots with horses and kickass jewelry. Would love to get to know you better!"

What was that? I thought. Strangest—and most unique—intro I'd ever heard, and I didn't even know what business she was there to represent. I was intrigued, and maybe that was her plan.

At the end of the meeting, I walked up to Becky and introduced myself. "You win the award for the most unique intro ever shared at a networking event," I told her.

"Thanks," she said. "I try." And her ruby red lipstick shone brighter as a smile spread across her face.

We agreed to meet for coffee the next week. I thought I might hear that she sells the jewelry she wore or maybe even the boots, but I was off base with both assumptions. Becky had once been a successful corporate leader with teams all over the country. Prior to motherhood, her weeks were full of flights, strategy sessions, and business growth meetings. When her first child was eighteen months old, she decided to leave corporate America and begin a different job, that of a stay-at-home mom.

Over a delicious cup of cucumber mint tea, I learned Becky's kids were five and seven years old. I also found out she didn't enjoy the life she'd created. She loved the privilege she had to be at home for the kids' firsts; she loved homework time and adventures with them; she loved the family dinners she and her husband enjoyed with the kids every night. It seemed most of the stay-at-home mom thing worked for her, but I could tell there was something missing.

Becky used to lead large teams, and when she switched gears to stay home with her kids, her team became very small—and not only in terms of height. She longed to lead more than her household and children. She wanted to showcase her leadership abilities and had begun to do so in other ways. She joined the PTA at her kids' school and got involved in the clubs they were part of. She thought her past professional experience would be beneficial in these arenas.

> **❝She longed to lead more than her household and children.❞**

Unfortunately, the other moms involved in these groups thought Becky's ideas were too out there. Her fundraiser idea for the PTA that could have brought in ten thousand dollars was pushed aside for the traditional fundraiser known to bring in a solid fifteen hundred.

"I can see the other moms cringe when I speak at the meetings. I just don't get it. My ideas are solid. They work. And yet time and time again, they're dismissed. I've begun to make excuses for who I am and shrink back rather than stand up as strong leaders do, the way I used to. In all honesty, I go to networking meetings—like the one at which we met—just so I can be the real me. I'm bold. I'm creative. I'm a lot for some people, but that's who I am," she explained.

This was a perfect opportunity to share my Baskin-Robbins pink spoon story. I'm a big fan of the pink spoons; they allow me to sample different ice cream flavors until

I find the one I most want to order each time I visit. All of their thirty-one flavors aren't going to appeal to everyone, the same way we're not everyone's favorite flavor. Just because we don't pick a particular flavor doesn't mean that flavor doesn't deserve to be there.

Our conversation that day was vulnerable, heartfelt, and much needed. Becky's not everyone's favorite flavor. Neither am I. But rather than make excuses for who we are and how we show up in the world, we encouraged each other to ditch those excuses and show up as our true selves.

I saw Becky a few months later in the same networking group where we first met. She was excited to catch me up on some exciting news. She had created a four-week program for kids to encourage them to be their unique selves, and she was given the opportunity to lead the program with different grade levels in her kids' school. She also shared that she and her family now made Baskin-Robbins part of their weekly routine, with the goal to pick a different flavor each time they visit.

QUESTION TO CONSIDER
What excuses do you make in your life?
How would it feel to ditch them all and go
after what you want?

ACTION TO IMPLEMENT
Go on an Excuse Diet

- Write one goal you've wanted to accomplish for some time.
- Under the goal, write "Reasons," along with the actual reasons you haven't yet achieved the goal.
- Mark a big X through "Reasons" and instead write "Excuses."
- Now mark a big X through all of your excuses, and create your plan to achieve your goal.
- Bonus: If your excuse diet leaves you hungry, go to Baskin-Robbins for a few pink spoon samples. They'll be delicious and will also remind you of the pink spoon lesson!

_____

_____

_____

_____

_____

CHAPTER 26

Focus on Your Wins

"Winning isn't everything, but wanting it is."
—*ARNOLD PALMER*

"What were your wins** this week?" The first time I heard that question, my mind went blank. It was my first coach who had asked it.

"My wins?" I asked.

"Yeah," he said. "What went well for you this week?"

It seemed like hours went by as I scanned my brain for something positive. A client canceled her session with me. I got stuck over an hour in construction traffic. The number on the scale didn't say what I wanted it to say. I'd had a cold for over a week. I wasn't sure where I was supposed to find these wins.

I replied to his question with one weak answer. "The weather's better."

"There you go!" he exclaimed. "Now tell me about that. It's been rainy and chilly where I'm at, so I'd love to hear more about the weather where you are."

As I described the rising temps and our second day of sunshine, I wondered how this was supposed to help me build my business, the main reason I'd hired this coach.

After I answered the wins question every week for several months, I learned that a focus on the positive is a key step in the creation of a successful business—or a successful marriage or a successful life, in general. I believe this so much that I now greet many of my own clients with the same question. "What were your wins this week?"

Scientists say we have sixty thousand thoughts that run through our brains every day, and of those sixty thousand, eighty to ninety percent are negative. We are wired to find what's wrong in the world far more often than we are to look for what's right.

Think of the news. The top stories always have to do with war, murder, natural disasters, missing persons, and politicians who don't always behave well. The feel-good stories always come later in the broadcast, as if they're somehow less important.

Social media follows the same theme. People tell their social media "friends" about the fight with their spouse that morning or the electric company who did them wrong or the mother-in-law they'll never speak to again.

Our brains find it normal to scan for the negatives in the world.

On June 9, 2015, my brain was busy in its quest to find the negative. Our daughter had moved back in with us after her cancer diagnosis, and this was the day she walked upstairs with a clump of hair in her hand. She said in an even tone, "Today's the day. It's time for the hair to go."

She'd begun to lose her long, thick hair just after her chemo sessions began, first in strands and then in large clumps. She read that if she got it cut to a shorter length, it might not fall out as fast, so she'd already gone from hair down her back to chin-length hair.

"Will you shave it off?" she asked.

"Of course," I answered in a calm way, just as I used to when she'd ask if I'd make her favorite meal for dinner.

I walked to our laundry room, stood on my tiptoes, and reached for the familiar black box, the one that had lived in our laundry room cabinet for the past twenty years. I'd used the clippers inside that box countless times to give my two sons their summer haircuts, the kind that don't require a comb for the months of June, July, and August.

This time was different. This time I grabbed them from the top shelf so I could remove one of my daughter's identifying features. From the time she was a toddler, people would stop us to compliment her and admire her thick mane.

I felt the sting of tears in the corners of my eyes as I began the process. We didn't speak during this ceremony neither of us wanted to have. When I finished, she went downstairs to shower, and I cleaned up the hair that had fallen to the floor. I allowed a clump of it to run through my fingers in an attempt to bring back the memories of ponytails, braids, and bows. Instead, all I felt was a foreign substance that was dry and straw-like.

> **❝We didn't speak during this ceremony neither of us wanted to have.❞**

When I heard her turn off the water, I pulled myself together so she wouldn't notice how much I'd been affected by this new, unwelcome haircut. She came upstairs with a slight grin on her face. *What could she have to be happy about?* I thought.

"You know," she said, "this whole bald thing—what a time and money saver. No more drying and curling my hair, and shampoo can be eliminated from my Target list altogether."

And there it was. A win in the midst of what I'd have considered an epic loss.

Our next win came later that year when her PET scan showed no sign of cancer, and in the fall of 2020, we will celebrate the biggest win of all: five years cancer-free.

QUESTION TO CONSIDER
**How often do you focus on your wins?
How can you increase that frequency?**

ACTION TO IMPLEMENT
Toss Your L Column and Celebrate Your W's

- Begin a Win Journal.
  - ° At the end of each day, make a list of three wins you experienced that day.
  - ° Add the date to each entry.
  - ° Every quarter, pour yourself your favorite drink, sit in your favorite chair, and read your wins from the past three months. Relive the memories, feel all the good feelings, and smile at the incredible life you have.

_____

_____

_____

_____

_____

_____

_____

_____

_____

_____

CHAPTER 27

Teach Your Brain Some New Tricks

"You have power over your mind, not outside events. Realize this and you will find strength."
—MARCUS AURELIUS

I'm sure you've heard the well-known saying, "You can't teach an old dog new tricks." Each time I hear the saying, it's followed by an example of how someone *did* teach an old dog (or an old cat or a set-in-her-ways colleague) a new trick. It's possible to do. It's just not always easy.

When I grew weary of my checklist life, I wanted to learn the trick to living a different and better life. I saw other people do it. They were fulfilled and content both in their personal and professional lives. Unfortunately, I didn't know how to make that happen for myself. The checklist life was all I'd ever known. It was a compilation of how I was raised, what I'd learned through my observations of others for many years, and how I was built on the inside—what some people call personality. I thought I was stuck, and that thought, of course, did nothing to get me to a better place.

I look back at that time in my life when I tried to figure out who I was, what I wanted, and how to rid myself of what I didn't want, and realize now I may have looked like a dog who tried to learn a new trick. The new trick for me was learning to manage my mind and understand that my life was all in my control. Remember, I was the Empress of Excuses, and I looked to my external world when things didn't go well in my life when I should have looked where I had the ability to change it—internally.

When I began to work with my client Lynette, she, too, was on an external excursion to figure out how to change the people and situations around her. She led a sales and marketing department for a local construction business, and she was passionate about the work she did and the results she and her team achieved. She stood out in her male-dominated industry as a girl who got things done, and she communicated well with her colleagues and customers in an effort to be as effective as possible in her role.

She came to me after months of frustration. She told me she felt shut down by the male owners of the business

she worked for. She shared that she'd always been a creative force on the leadership team but had begun to feel
that her ideas were ignored and sometimes even mocked.
She hung in there for a while and tried not to let it get to
her, but when she realized her challenges at work had
begun to affect her relationships at home, she reached
out for help.

"I've always been one to give a hundred and fifty percent in all I do," she told me. "Since things have become
tense at work, I come in earlier. I stay later. I prepare for
meetings like crazy so I've got innovative ideas to share.
And yet the more I do to try to overcome the hurdles in
front of me, the more I fall flat on my face."

I could see the anxiety on Lynette's face and then
the sadness. "The stress has gotten to me. Tension at
home is high because I put so much into my job but I
neglect things at home. I feel like my husband should
understand. He doesn't make this any easier, and I don't
want him to tell me to calm down anymore. How can
I calm down when my job may be on the line? I used
to have such a strong relationship with my bosses, but
they've changed. They're close-minded just like my husband has been. Even my kids push my buttons, and they
used to be my respite from any part of my life I had trou-
ble with."

When Lynette finally got it all out, her shoulders
sagged, and her face showed a look of defeat.

> **"When she finished, her shoulders sagged, and her face showed a look of defeat."**

I recognized my past self in Lynette. She focused on external people and situations for changes she wanted to see in her life. She needed her bosses to accept her ideas. She needed her husband to be more compassionate and empathetic. She needed her kids to freeze in time until she could get herself back on track, back to the place where she felt whole.

The reality was that none of what Lynette needed could be found externally. The secret to all she needed was within her. She and I worked together for a year, and over the course of that time, she moved her focus from a change in external forces to an internal focus on herself. She learned to manage her thoughts and feelings so they'd prompt her into beneficial actions. She taught that "old" brain of hers some new tricks.

Several months into our time together, Lynette accepted a leadership position with another organization, one that is also in a male-dominated industry. She didn't let her past experiences put any sort of blemish on her thoughts about her talents as a leader. She thrived in her new role and immersed herself in the new industry, her company, and her team.

Lynette learned to use her "new" brain to allow her to live her best life, and the tricks she learned worked both professionally and personally. I was honored to be part of her transformation and laughed along with her the day she told me, "Who says you can't teach an old dog new tricks? 'Woof, woof' to those who claim you can't!"

QUESTION TO CONSIDER
What new tricks would you love to teach your brain? What old tricks do you want to delete from it?

ACTION TO IMPLEMENT
Get Your Magic Wand Ready
- Write down a challenge that keeps you awake at night.
- Under the challenge, write down the obstacles in the way of it being overcome.
- Cross out any obstacles listed that are outside of yourself.
- Focus on the obstacles over which you have control.
- Devise a plan to teach your brain the new trick to overcome those obstacles.

_____

_____

_____

CHAPTER 28

Slow Down the Checklist Ride

"Slow down and enjoy life. It's not only the scenery you miss by going too fast; you also miss the sense of where you are going and why."
—EDDIE CANTOR

As I get older, I've noticed changes in myself—and I don't just mean the additional wrinkles that pop up (or experience lines, as some like to call them). It's that I no longer care about some of the things that used to get so much of my attention.

For years, I was an every-Saturday-morning house cleaner. Maybe when the house was full of our kids—and often their friends—it was messier than it is now. I just know that now the dust on the end tables and the dishes in the dish drainer don't affect me like they once did. The fingerprints left by our grandkids on our sliding glass door stay on that glass much longer than I'd ever have allowed them to stay when the prints belonged to my kids. Now I look at those little handprints, and my heart swells.

The checklist ride is a speedy one, and once you hop on, it's not easy to put on the brakes. Jess sped into my client base as a young, successful entrepreneur, wife, and mom to three children under the age of five. She talked fast, she moved fast, and she burned out fast.

> **"The checklist ride is a speedy one, and once you hop on, it's not easy to put on the brakes."**

The source of the burnout was a business problem many would like to have. Her business had such rapid expansion she felt like she couldn't keep up with its growth and also balance everything else in her life.

What started out as a social media experiment—healthy shakes and juices with fast, free delivery to homes and businesses—had turned into two storefronts and an ecommerce website. From hardcore health nuts to busy business professionals to stay-at-home moms who wanted a refreshing, quick way to get their vitamins and minerals, Jess had found the secret many people wanted.

The problem was she couldn't provide what she needed for herself, and she felt the shift in her physical and emotional well-being. She told me she'd decided to hire a coach to help her with time and priority management: "I just have too much on my plate, and I'm worried I will miss something. Can you help me get better organized?"

While I do provide this type of coaching, I realized after our first session there was something else Jess might need more. I admired her attitude about her work and life, in general. She had two failed businesses before she launched the current successful one, and her mindset was that of fail, learn, fail, learn, succeed—a mindset I wished I'd learned as early in life as she had.

Jess understood the best things in life come as a result of what we learn from the failures we experience. She also knew how important it is to do what we say we'll do, honor our commitments, and not let people down.

There was one person Jess was letting down—Jess herself. She was an athlete for most of her life, and it was important to her that she stay active. When she became a mother, it wasn't as easy to get time on her own for a run or the strength training she'd always loved, but she did what she could. When her business exploded, her "Jess time" was nowhere to be seen, and its absence took a toll on her well-being.

Jess's checklist ride moved at a thrilling pace, but she felt the effects of having no pit stops along the way.

As we worked on her calendar and her many weekly commitments, I suggested she add another one.

"Let's discuss how you can add time blocks each week for your physical health," I said.

Through the phone line I heard . . . nothing. And the nothingness on that line seemed to last forever. Then, I heard a quiet, "Are you serious?"

"Well, yes," I replied. "What comes up when you think of that possibility?"

Her voice quivered in her reply. "How do I do that? I don't have time for what's on my plate now, and you want me to add more?"

Jess didn't understand it wasn't about the addition of another task. It was about how that addition would help slow down her checklist ride.

Fast forward a few months and Jess had not only found a way to add strength training and running to her weekly schedule, she'd also added time each morning to stretch, pray, and write in her journal. It was the slowdown she needed to keep up with everything else she wanted to accomplish.

She didn't add more hours to her day. She didn't set her alarm any earlier. Jess realized when she slowed down her ride and took care of herself first, she was able to accomplish more than she'd ever imagined she could.

QUESTION TO CONSIDER
What parts of your life move so fast you can't keep up?

ACTION TO IMPLEMENT
Pump the Brakes

- Choose one of the areas you identified above where you feel you can't keep up.
- List your reasons why that area moves too fast for you.
- Under each reason, determine what influence you have over a slowdown or elimination of it altogether.
- What feelings does the slowdown or elimination evoke?
- What actions do those feelings prompt you to take?
- When will you commit to take those actions?

_____

_____

_____

_____

_____

_____

CHAPTER 29

FLATTEN YOUR FEAR

"Each of us must confront our own fears, must come face to face with them. How we handle our fears will determine where we go with the rest of our lives. To experience adventure or to be limited by the fear of it."
—JUDY BLUME

To me, **fear is** like a dark room in an unfamiliar house. I'm in the room and feel my way around for the flashlight I know is there. I bump into something and trip. Now I'm on the floor, and I feel something fuzzy. Is it a rug? Is it a stuffed animal? Is it a real animal? And if it's real, does it have sharp teeth? All I want is to flood that room with light. If only I could find my flashlight.

The dark room is what I fear. The flashlight is the courage I need to push myself through that fear. That flashlight is what I needed most when I decided to leave my checklist life, and Laura was in the same boat.

Laura worked for an organization that hired me to provide team development services. I shared team trust information on my first day there. Of the fifteen people in the room, Laura was one who stood out to me. She smiled nonstop. She nodded at appropriate times and added affirmative statements like, "Yes, I so agree." It was as if every word I shared soaked into the very fiber of her being. I thought I'd enjoy my work with Laura. I also made the assumption she spent some of her free time on personal development due to her great interest in what I shared.

I scheduled time the following week to meet individually with several team members. "I'm the OG here," Laura told me during our meeting. "I've been here longer than anyone else on the team—eighteen years. My boss, Rob, started here five years ago in my department, and I trained him. He was promoted, and now I report to him."

I listened to Laura's tone. I wondered how she felt about his rise through the ranks while she remained in the same role throughout her tenure with the company. Her tone gave nothing away. Then she mentioned something that caught my attention. "Can you repeat that, please?" I asked.

"Oh, yeah," she said. "I forgot you're new around here. You're not used to how we communicate. Everyone else is. What I said was that Rob did what he always does after last week's staff meeting. He called me out in front of everyone for something he felt I'd miscommunicated to the client. When I said something to him as we all left the meeting, he mumbled under his breath and walked down the hall. I'm so sick of his weasel behaviors. He's the leader, and he thinks he can mumble and walk away from me? I don't think so. I yelled down the hall at him, and then the weasel turned into a piranha. We had a back-and-forth screaming match until he gave up and walked away. You'll learn soon enough there's nothing unusual about this. It's the norm for Rob and me. He doesn't respect me, and I don't respect him."

This vision of her screaming at her boss didn't match what I'd seen in Laura in that initial team trust session, but since this was my first private session with her, I decided to listen and wait to learn more.

Over the next few weeks, I learned that Laura knew her stuff. Others came to her with problems because they knew she'd have viable solutions. Her vast experience made her an expert on the team. Her relationship with Rob, however, made her resentful and often unapproachable to others.

Laura shared that she was a single mom to four daughters ranging in age from sixteen to twenty-three.

The divorce from their dad hadn't been amicable, and Laura seemed to have residual negative feelings from that experience. She told me it was all on her shoulders to support her family, and even though her relationship with her boss made her feel stressed, overwhelmed, and insecure, she had to keep the job.

That "had to" sounded familiar to me. It had a ring of, "I live a checklist life, and the checklist says I must continue to do things long after they bring me joy." Yes, I knew that "had to" well. It was the fear that held me hostage in my own checklist life for far too long.

> **"That "had to" sounded familiar to me. It had a ring of, "I live a checklist life, and the checklist says I must continue to do things long after they bring me joy."**

As we got to know each other better, Laura admitted she put a wall up in an effort to protect herself from additional hurt. When Rob didn't show her respect, her wall delivered jabs to him. When her coworkers wanted one too many things from her, her wall delivered terse, arrogant answers. And Laura confessed the wall wasn't just around her at work. She did the same thing in her personal relationships. She didn't allow anyone to get too close to her. The wall was Laura's dark room, and she needed a flashlight.

One day, I asked Laura if I could connect with her on LinkedIn. "Oh, I don't have a LinkedIn profile," she told me. "I've been with the company so long I don't see the point. I know people use it to network and find jobs, but I don't have a need for either."

I shared with her the many benefits of LinkedIn and was pleased when I received a connection invitation from her a week later.

As Laura built her professional network, her personal one also grew. She told me she began to socialize more in her free time and stress less. I could see it in her. The weight of her time in that dark room had made her sluggish, resentful, and distant. As she found her flashlight and pushed her way through the fear she experienced, she seemed lighter, happier, and so much more engaged.

Laura's relationship with her boss was one area of her life that didn't improve. Perhaps there was too much bad history between them. After my time with the organization had finished, I learned Laura had been terminated. It was the way I found out that made me smile, though. I received a LinkedIn update about Laura's new role and had to look twice when I noticed the organization was also a new one. I sent my congrats to her and almost instantly received a reply.

"It happened," she said. "He fired me. Had it not been for your guidance and support, I never would have had the courage to walk out that day and find the perfect job for me. I'm now able to make use of my strengths and

experience every day in an environment where my contri-
butions are valued. It feels different. It feels good." And as
I read her message, I completed her thoughts in my mind.
"My world is brighter now that I've found my flashlight."

QUESTION TO CONSIDER
How does fear hold you back in your life?
What might it feel like when you find your
own flashlight?

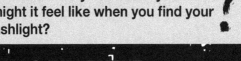

ACTION TO IMPLEMENT
Turn on the Light
- Complete this statement: The one area where
  fear holds me back the most is _____.
- Now picture yourself in that dark room.
- What is the flashlight you need to shine a light
  on your fear? Is it courage to:
  ° Have a difficult conversation with a loved one?
  ° Update your resumé?
  ° Go for that promotion?
  ° Leave a relationship?
- When you determine what your flashlight is,
  it's time to create your action plan to find the
  light to get you there!

_____

_____

_____

CHAPTER 30

Halt the Busy Train

"Take a deep breath. Get present in the moment and ask yourself what is important this very second."
—GREGORY MCKEOWN

"Hey, how are you doing?"

"Busy!"

I hear that answer so often in the course of a week that I think "busy" is the new "fine." It's an automatic answer for many, and it was a badge of honor I wore for many years of my life. I stayed busy, which allowed me to keep up with my checklist.

I saw it as a competition. When it comes to sports or board games, I'm not competitive, but in my checklist life, I wanted to win. How many items on my checklist could I complete in the least amount of time?

I gave birth to my third child at the age of twenty-three and thought I deserved a blue ribbon (and not just because she was almost ten and a half pounds). I thought I was a winner because I viewed myself as successful in my race through life. I went as fast as I could and checked off boxes all along the way while I stayed—you guessed it—busy.

My busy-ness was the buffer I used to numb my real feelings. Some people buffer with food, alcohol, drugs, shopping, or gambling. I buffered with busy-ness. If I could check off all the boxes in the least amount of time, I'd win the race.

I remember the year I stopped my work as a fourth-grade teacher and moved to third grade. I switched schools and found myself on a team much larger than the one I'd left. I became fast friends with a fellow third-grade teacher who was around my age. She was single and enjoyed her social life. I was in my early thirties with three kids who kept me busy from sunup to sundown.

One Monday as we ate lunch in the teacher's lounge, she shared with the rest of the group what she'd done over the weekend. She told us about a concert, a date, some shopping, and brunch with the girls.

I thought about my weekend and didn't say a word. I listened as others shared the fun they'd had. At one point, my new teaching buddy pointed at me. "How about you?" she asked. "What did you do over the weekend?"

"Not much," I replied. "Definitely not as much as you did."

Based on her repeated questions, I learned my non-answer wouldn't work with this group. Everyone at the table looked at me, and I tried to come up with a way to make my weekend sound as exciting and carefree as everyone else's.

I don't lie well, and this trait often works in my favor, but in this case, it was quite difficult to share what my weekend had included. "Well," I began, "on Saturday I did laundry most of the day because all three kids are involved in extracurricular activities so we have their day-time clothes, their uniforms, and then the after-game clothes. On Sunday I did my normal 'get meals ready for the week' routine."

"What do you mean?" my new teacher friend asked. "You went to the grocery store?"

"Yes, but that's just step one. After I get the groceries for the week, I make meals for the upcoming week. The ground beef I buy might be for burgers on Sunday, but then I'll use some for spaghetti sauce or meatloaf or tacos. I get all the meals ready so the week is easier. Sundays are busy, but it's worth it Monday through Friday."

"Oh my," she whispered. "I just leave work each day and go to the store to buy something for my dinner that night. Now that I know how you spend your weekends, I'm not sure we can be friends."

Everyone at the table broke out in belly laughs. She'd made a joke, of course, but I had to force my own laugh. I felt like I was the center of her joke, and for me the checklist life wasn't fun and games. It was serious business.

> **"I felt like I was the center of her joke, and for me the checklist life wasn't fun and games."**

I was busy. I'd already checked off so many boxes that she hadn't even begun. I was way ahead of her. I was the winner of the competition. The problem was no one else cared about the competition.

I didn't halt my busy train after that conversation in the teacher's lounge. I didn't halt it for many years. The checklist I worked to completion seemed to have a spell over me. "Stay busy, and you'll win, Tracy," it said to me each day.

As I continued to buffer with busy-ness, some important events happened. My kids graduated from grade school and then high school. They went off to college, began their careers, moved into their own homes, and started their families.

The checklist I held dear for so many years lost its hold on me, and I made a conscious decision to toss it out. Even after it was gone, I mentally relived those years when my house was full of kids who laughed and played, and I wished the checklist had floated away long before it did.

I no longer thought my checklist was the way. I realized it had only gotten in the way. And what I'd always heard, but understood far too late, is so very true: the days are long but the years are oh, so short.

QUESTION TO CONSIDER
What competition do you find yourself in that doesn't serve you well?

ACTION TO IMPLEMENT
Check That Speedometer
- As you work to halt your busy train, list thoughts you have about what others might think about your choice to do so.
- Now list what you'll make others' thoughts mean about you.
- Consider how you might change those stories you tell yourself that don't serve you well.

CHAPTER 31

Kick It Into Gear with Self-Confidence

"With realization of one's own potential and self-confidence in one's ability, one can build a better world."

—*DALAI LAMA*

People often use the terms "confidence" and "self-confidence" interchangeably. I've done this, too; that is, until I learned the important distinction between the terms.

Confidence is the belief you can do something because you've done it before. You have evidence that you can be successful, and that evidence doesn't come from continual wins. It really comes from your will to try, fail, and get up to try again. Eventually, we succeed, and our confidence muscle grows, much like a bodybuilder's biceps after regular workouts.

Self-confidence, on the other hand, is the belief you can do something you've never done before. It requires deliberate conviction and great focus on the thoughts needed to accomplish the great thing you've got your mind and heart set on.

Before Roberta and I began our work together, she told me she had not one ounce of self-confidence. She wasn't upset when she told me, and she didn't seem frustrated.

She stated matter-of-factly, "I started my business because I love bookkeeping. I know that sounds weird, but I do. I love the organization behind all of it, and I love that my clients can count on me to have all their ducks in a row—or, to be more precise, all of their financial transactions recorded without error."

Her face lit up as she described how much she enjoyed her work. But that light was short-lived. She followed up her excitement with a dose of vulnerability that cast a shadow over the light.

"I find accurate bookkeeping to be easy. When it comes to the growth of my business, though, that's anything but easy. I want to support more clients, but I don't want to go to networking events or post on social media. I am confident in my abilities as a bookkeeper. I have very satisfied clients. I have zero self-confidence as a business owner, though. I know it sounds silly, but I'd love for the clients to magically appear because I can't force myself to do the work needed to bring them on board."

I realized, of course, that Roberta's lack of self-confidence was a problem, but I was happy to hear she had self-awareness about the problem—the first step to get her to a better place.

While I've never been a bookkeeper, I had walked in Roberta's shoes in the Land of No Self-Confidence. My brain would tell me to stick with what I knew—my checklist life—because it was easy, it was what I was used to, it was what everyone expected of me, and it was, of course, a simpler path to take.

I think it's easy to develop confidence through positive results. The proof is there, and it pushes us forward to do more of the same. Our confidence grows with each level of success we achieve, and we nudge ourselves forward day after day.

When the proof isn't there, it's difficult to imagine it. How can I believe it will happen when I haven't experienced it yet? How can I feel certain of my own abilities to make it happen? How can I push myself forward when all I see in front of me is darkness? Confidence lights the way. Self-confidence requires that we feel our way through the darkness even when we don't know what boogeyman might be in our path.

ffHow can I believe it will happen when I haven't experienced it yet? How can I feel certain of my own abilities to make it happen?**JJ**

Roberta hired me to help her build her business, and we both knew the way to do that was to first establish her self-confidence. Contrary to popular opinion, we didn't start with actions she could take to build that self-confidence, because actions aren't what make the difference.

We started with her thoughts. In one of her coaching sessions, I asked her to share her "mean girl" thoughts with me. She came up with one: "You're not smart enough to own your own business."

"Okay," I said. "What else?" Silence. "What other 'mean girl' thoughts come to mind when you think of yourself as a business owner?" Silence.

I counted in my head from one to thirty. Then I counted all those numbers again backwards.

"What's up?" I asked. "You must have more. The mean girl in my brain is quite talkative."

"I can't," Roberta said. "I don't think I can do this. I don't see how I'll ever be able to believe something I don't have proof of. It's like I want to climb Mt. Everest, but my only shoes are flip-flops."

What a perfect comparison! She was right. As we build our self-confidence—that belief in our ability to do something before we've ever accomplished it—it's like mountain climbing in flip-flops. I laughed at her comparison, which also made Roberta laugh.

"I'm a flip-flop gal, too," I said. "Let's climb that mountain together." And we did. Week after week, and month after month, Roberta and I met. Her self-confidence grew, and she brought it with her to networking events, potential client meetings, and even the grocery store.

Roberta's business grew as her self-confidence did, and she often let me know she did her best bookkeeping work with flip-flops on her feet.

QUESTION TO CONSIDER
How would added self-confidence help
you in your personal and professional life?

ACTION TO IMPLEMENT
Believe It So You Can See It
- Think of three things you avoid because you
  don't believe you can achieve them.
- Write a best-case scenario for each. In a dream
  world, what would you have at your disposal in
  order to achieve those things?
- Consider how you can make some of your
  dream world a reality.

_____

_____

_____

_____

_____

_____

_____

_____

_____

CHAPTER 32

Build Your Boundaries

> *"Your personal boundaries protect the inner core of your identity and your right to choices."*
> —*GERARD MANLEY HOPKINS*

When I think of my childhood, I smile. I remember nightly family dinners together, parents who socialized on our patio with neighborhood couples, and nearby friends who were always ready for some fun. We spent our summers outside from the time we finished breakfast until the street lights came on at night, with quick breaks during the day for lunch and dinner. We were young, we were carefree, and we were quite creative with how we spent our time.

The neighborhood kids invented a game as summer turned to fall; we were a sight to see as we'd walk to our neighbor's leaf-filled yard with rakes in hand. Over the course of a Saturday morning, those rakes got some use as we created buildings with the leaves. There were exterior walls, doorways, interior rooms, and even sidewalks that led up to the leaf buildings. If an aerial view were possible, it would have looked like an architect's blueprint. For us, it was a way to set boundaries.

Kids will be kids, so it made perfect sense to me that my friends would be my helpers as we created the leaf masterpieces. Once the buildings were complete, those friends turned into foes as they weren't allowed in my leaf building, and I wasn't allowed in theirs. The fun creation of the leaf buildings morphed into yet another fun activity where we protected our fortresses. We'd wear our mean, "stay out of my building" faces, and seconds later we'd roll around in the leaves and giggle together.

If only boundary setting as an adult were as easy—and fun—as it was for me as a kid. When I first left my checklist life behind, I had people in my life who didn't understand my decisions. They were used to the way I'd always been and were wary of the person I started to become. As their antennae went up, I was tempted to fall right back into the familiar place I'd always been.

My friend Briana had similar challenges when she tried to break out of the mold she'd created for herself. "I'm like Julia Roberts in *Runaway Bride*," she told me one day as we walked for our physical health and talked for our emotional health.

"Ummm . . . what?" I asked.

"You know, the egg thing. Her character in the movie was engaged so many times, and then at the last minute, she'd run away from the man she was to marry. With each of her relationships, she adjusted to the preferences of her man. She realized one day she had no idea how she liked her eggs because she ate them however her fiancé at the time liked them. The scene where she was surrounded by eggs—scrambled, over easy, sunny side up, poached, hard boiled—it just brought me to tears. I do that, too. Not the egg thing, but with other things. I adjust to what everyone else wants because I don't want to be judged for my choices."

Briana's words hit me hard, and I thought about the life changes I'd made over the past few years. For how much of my life was I hesitant to make a change because of what someone else might think? How firm was I when I threw out my checklist and lived life without a pre-designed plan? And how well did I set my own boundaries in what I would and wouldn't accept from others? Better yet, did I set boundaries at all, or did I spend years in a wishy-washy life so others' needs were met?

"For how much of my life was I hesitant to make a change because of what someone else might think?"

I thought of the famous quote: "What other people think of you is none of your business." I shared it with Briana, and her eyes glistened with tears. "You're right," she said, "but how do I make myself not care about what they think?"

Our walk was a bit longer than normal that day. Sometimes we need more time to talk, so we get a bonus of more time to walk, too. Briana wanted to go back to school to become a graphic designer. Her current job paid well, but it stifled her creativity. She'd talked with her husband, mom, and sister about her graphic design dream, and they all told her she should stay put and collect those nice paychecks.

Together, while we added steps to our daily count, we created the plan for Briana to do the research on which school to attend, what it would cost, how she would pay for it, and how she'd share the news with her family about her graphic design program. The more we talked, the more eager Briana became. She walked a bit taller with each step of the plan in place because she knew she was ready for this new path. She prepared the boundaries she'd set to make it happen and was proud of herself for that courageous first step.

QUESTION TO CONSIDER
Where in your life do you eat everyone else's favorite eggs rather than stand up for what you most want?

ACTION TO IMPLEMENT
Draw That Line in the Sand

- Think of an area in your life where you go through the motions to meet others' expectations.
- Write down that example, along with what you'd prefer to do instead.
- Write a list of the people this change might affect.
- Write out the courageous conversation you will have with each of those people about the decision you've made and why you've made it.
- Schedule and conduct those conversations.
- Enjoy those newfound boundaries!

CHAPTER 33

Push Forward with an Accountability Partner

> *"A friend can inspire enthusiasm as well as accountability, and that serves to challenge you."*
> —*DEANNA COSSO AND ROMUALD ANDRADE, SUCCESS CLONING*

On a scale of one to ten, I give myself an eight when it comes to the discipline I practice with my time and commitments. If I tell myself I will mop the floor or create the training program or vacuum the car, it's as good as done. That strength of discipline makes simple tasks easy for me to commit to and complete.

It's the bigger undertakings that have been troublesome for me because it's so much easier to fall back to the path of least resistance, that checklist for life, than it is to catapult my way through the mucky mess of a big change.

My career 3.0 in corporate training felt like I had gotten rid of my checklist life for good. I learned something new—something that was exciting and different—and I got to do all the best parts. The training company I subbed my services through did all of the pre-work for me. They marketed their training programs, talked with interested organizations, negotiated their pricing, and got clients to sign on the dotted line. My role was simple: show up with an attitude of inspiration and encouragement for the groups I worked with each day.

My adult learning toolbox began to fill up, and I was engaged in the world of professional development. I helped leaders communicate and lead in the most effective ways they could. I loved the work and believed my checklist and I had broken up for good.

There was another side to the sub-contractor gig, though. The groups I worked with weren't my clients. They were the clients of the training company that hired me. This meant I had the opportunity to get them fired up for one or two days, but then I packed my bag and moved on to the next training gig. With each organization I helped and then left, I hoped they'd implement what we'd worked on during our time together. Given my history as an educator, this never felt good. I wanted to know what positive changes happened as a result of the work we did together. The work felt like an open loop for me, and I always wanted to close it.

My travel schedule as a corporate trainer had me in the northern portion of the country in the dead of winter, so I learned what UP meant when I traveled to Michigan in January. The Upper Peninsula felt like Antarctica to me, and I slept in my cold hotel room bundled up in two layers of clothing. I locked both locks on every hotel door, and sometimes I barricaded the door with the little desk in the room as an added security measure when the hotel looked questionable. Thank goodness no fires ever occurred because a quick escape would have been impossible.

I sat on countless airplanes while they de-iced and later announced the weather was too bad to fly. Many people complained about air travel, but I decided it was my favorite. On a plane, I could rely on the qualified pilot to get me to my next destination. When my travel itinerary called for a rental car instead, I was the person behind the wheel in the snow and ice. I'd hold the steering wheel so tight my fingers would get numb, and a lot of prayers were said on those drives.

I followed the motto of postal workers: "Neither snow nor rain nor heat nor gloom of night stays these couriers from the swift completion of their appointed rounds." My job was to be in the next city, ready to go at 7:00 a.m. the next day. If I made it to that next city by 6:45 a.m. after I drove all night in horrendous weather, I'd completed my part of the deal. Who needed sleep, right?

One winter night in Michigan, I called my husband to let him know I'd arrived and was safe. "I'm here," I said. "The flight arrived four hours late due to the blizzard, but my suitcase didn't make it on the flight."

"What's your plan?" he asked. "I know you didn't wear a business suit on your flight, so what will you wear tomorrow?"

"Oh, it gets better," I told him. "The next flight is due to arrive at 1:00 a.m., and I need to drive back to the airport to get my bag. They said they'd deliver it, but it wouldn't get here at the hotel until noon tomorrow."

My husband earned the Spouse of the Year title when he told me everything would work out. As he talked, I wiped away tears on my end of the phone. "This isn't what I wanted," I said. "I have to change my life—again."

He got to keep his Spouse of the Year trophy when he told me, "Then do it. If anyone can, it's you."

My husband is my soft place to fall. He is my never-ending cheerleader. He supports me and my ability to overcome challenges. He's not, however, the person to guide me through those challenges every step of the way. I knew I needed someone to hold a mirror up to show me how I was sabotaging myself. For that, I knew I needed a coach, so not long after that business trip from hell, I hired my first coach. He was my accountability partner in ways my husband couldn't be.

I wanted to end my crazy business travel. I reduced my availability to that client and began networking in my home area. I spoke at countless luncheons to get my name out there. I created social media posts and asked my faithful followers to share them with their friends. I did it all until the day I told the training company I was no longer available to cover work for them. And when they tried to swing a deal with me, I stood my ground.

> **❝I look back now and wonder if I ever would have cut off that relationship without the help of my accountability partner/coach.❞**

I look back now and wonder if I ever would have cut off that relationship without the help of my accountability partner/coach. It's so much easier to hang on for dear life, even when what we hang onto is another version of the checklist we no longer want.

My first coach's importance in my life is immeasurable as someone whose support came at a time I needed it most. I know without his guidance and gentle push off the proverbial cliff, I would have stayed stuck in another version of my checklist life. For the push he provided, I am forever grateful.

QUESTION TO CONSIDER
How would an accountability partner help you achieve the goals you've set for yourself?

ACTION TO IMPLEMENT
Partner Up for Amazing Results
- Make a list of at least five adults in your life that you admire and respect.
- Next to each name, write why that person would be a good accountability partner for you.
- Decide what each person could help you achieve.
- Rank those achievements and the people next to them in the order you'd like to begin.
- Have a courageous conversation with Potential Accountability Partner Number One!

_____

_____

_____

_____

_____

_____

_____

CHAPTER 34

Champion Your Most Desired Changes

"You never change your life until you step out of your comfort zone; change begins at the end of your comfort zone."
—ROY T. BENNETT

everal years ago, a friend of mine shared that a mutual friend had decided to champion a young girl in our hometown. "What's that?" I asked.

"Pam decided to champion Sophie," she repeated. I'm quite sure it was the blank look on my face that prompted her to go further. "You know, she supports her, advocates for her, mentors her. Sophie didn't have the best role models when she grew up, so Pam stepped up and now helps in any ways she can as Sophie gets through the last of her high school years."

This was a new term for me. I'd never heard it before. A champion? Of course, I knew the champion was the winner of the race or the game or the tournament, but to champion a person? I guess the old adage is true. We do learn something new every day.

I was reminded of the term when I first met with Sarah, who was in need of a champion herself. She told me she had two jobs: her "real" job and her part-time job she worked in the evening. She was married, had four kids who ranged in age from eight to twenty, and she was a foster mom to both children and dogs.

She reached out to me for guidance with interview skills, as there was a position available in her workplace that interested her. She told me the new job would include about fifty percent travel, and she knew if she were offered the job, her work days would get longer than they already were. She was a bit nervous about what that would mean for her second job, since she worked there up to three evenings per week.

We met twice each week for a month to get her ready, putting her skills to the test in mock interviews. I noted Sarah's answers, body language, and perceived confidence. We also discussed how this job would impact her life for a short time each session.

I asked her one day why she worked two jobs. She'd made it clear to me in the prior session that the job wasn't needed for financial reasons. "I don't know," she answered. "I think I just like when I have a lot to do. Between the kids, the animals, the housework, and my two jobs, I don't have time to complain or worry about things that don't go well in my life."

When I asked about the travel aspect of the job, Sarah shared that it both excited and depressed her. "I've never traveled for work before, so it would be something new for me. I know I'll miss the kids, though, and I wouldn't be able to keep my evening job since I'd be gone so much. I don't know what that would mean for my fostering responsibilities. I may have to give that up for now—although just the thought of that makes me sad."

I noticed that as she moved full steam ahead with the idea of taking this new job, she hadn't spent much time at all focused on how it would affect her life as a whole. It seemed the travel and added hours she'd work would keep her in the busy zone so she didn't have to think about things she didn't want to think about.

Sarah's checklist was all about busy-ness. The more she piled on her plate, the more numb she became to the noise—or unpleasantries—in her life.

A couple of weeks after our last coaching session, I received a call from Sarah. "I got it," she said. "They offered me the job."

"Oh, Sarah! Congratulations!"

"I didn't accept it."

I thought my ears had played a trick on me. "What?" I asked.

"And that's not all," she continued. "I quit my second job, too."

It's not often that I'm speechless, but I must admit that I wasn't sure what to say about the news she'd shared. All I could muster was, "Hmmm . . ."

> **❝It's not often that I'm speechless, but I must admit that I wasn't sure what to say about the news she'd shared.❞**

Sarah went on. "I realized I've pushed for the wrong things in my life. My job is fine. I don't dislike it. My kids and four-legged friends? They're incredible. And don't even get me started on that man I married, who has held down the fort at home all this time I've scurried about to find my mojo everywhere but right here at home with him. I didn't even realize what I've wanted all along was to be more present with the family he and I have made together. I want to thank you for your help with interview skills and also for the questions you asked that no one else ever had. You helped me see the changes I'd chased weren't the ones I wanted or needed after all."

I hung up the phone, still speechless, and realized that being a champion for another person wasn't only a new concept for me; it was also a privilege.

QUESTION TO CONSIDER
Who can you champion in an effort to improve that person's life, as well as your own? How can you get started?

ACTION TO IMPLEMENT
Advocate the Life You Want to Live
- Visualize yourself as your own champion.
- How does this make you:
  - Think?
  - Feel?
  - Act?
- If you were able to think, feel, and act those ways every day, write the results you'd be able to achieve.
- Now visualize your life after you've achieved those results.

CHAPTER 35

Make Life Your Own Magnificent Marathon

"Grit is living life like it's a marathon, not a sprint."
—ANGELA DUCKWORTH

I am not a runner. Brisk walks are more my jam, but to those who run the full 26.2 miles of a marathon, I tip my hat to you. What an accomplishment!

Although I'll probably never cross a marathon finish line, I do enjoy looking at life as that kind of race, and I've set an intention to let go of my checklist life for good.

I've heard that some runners set two goals: one is for a good race day, and the other is a backup plan in case it's not a great running day. I've incorporated this mindset in my own life.

When I left teaching to begin my work in the business world, I thought my plan was set. I would work until I earned my court reporting certificate, which would bring the great flexibility I wanted. That plan didn't work out, but rather than give up on my marathon, I created a new plan. I started my corporate training journey, which then led me to start my coaching and team development business.

Many runners also download a training plan. There's an app for almost everything these days, and marathon running plans are no exception. They take the runner step by step through their training to prepare for the actual race.

Years ago, I created my checklist for life. This was pre-internet so there was nothing to download, but my brain and my life experiences took on the task on their own. I finally decided the checklist wasn't what I wanted as a guidepost for my life so I "downloaded" a new plan.

My new strategy included things my checklist didn't: vulnerability, authenticity, and the knowledge that when I fail it doesn't mean I'm wrong to try, but rather that I learn and grow through each failure.

My favorite tip gained from an experienced marathoner is to enjoy every moment. Marathoners take over fifty thousand steps to reach that finish line. It's difficult, I imagine, to enjoy every one of them, but I've learned how to do so in my life.

> **❝Marathoners take over fifty thousand steps to reach that finish line. It's difficult, I imagine, to enjoy every one of them, but I've learned how to do so in my life.❞**

When I take early morning walks in the town I've lived in since birth, I don't see my surroundings as an uninteresting blur. I breathe in the fresh air and focus on the blue sky decorated with fluffy clouds. I notice the little touches people add to their homes—a front door painted a unique color, landscaping in the peak of its bloom, toys left outside from the night before which results in a flood of memories of my child-rearing years. I soak it all in. I enjoy every moment.

And this doesn't only happen on those morning walks. I notice the changes I've implemented since I threw away my checklist life. In those years, life moved fast. Do a task. Check the box. Do the next task. Check the next box. No time to slow down. No time for a pit stop. Keep at it. Day in and day out. Check those boxes. Go, go, go!

Now I'm intentional about how I spend my time. There are days I'm busy, but I'm busy with work I love, what I was put on this earth to do. I coach women to let go of their feelings of overwhelm and low self-worth. I speak on stages to help my audiences see that a checklist life isn't the right plan for any of us. I work with teams in organizations to help them lead from the heart. I live my passion and enjoy every moment of it.

I often wonder what I'd tell my younger self if I could go back and do so. That younger version of me was fast-moving, competitive, and sheltered inside the wall she built around herself. She cared a lot about what other people thought of her—even when she claimed she didn't. She second-guessed herself and wished that things could be different.

When she finally realized that life wasn't about the checklist, she stepped into a new version of herself. Her confidence rose. The competition to have the most complete checklist faded away. Her vulnerability took center stage.

So what is it that I'd tell that younger version of myself? Be patient, Tracy. Your life isn't a sprint; it's a marathon. And in that marathon, you might get some blisters on your toes, but you'll also have the magnificent opportunity to celebrate along the way, to enjoy every moment. You don't have to, of course, but since you have the opportunity, why wouldn't you?

About the Author

racy Bianco is a leadership coach, trainer, and speaker. As the founder and CEO of Bright Side Training Solutions, she is passionate about helping others understand they are leaders—of work teams, of their families, of themselves.

Throughout her career, Tracy has had the privilege of leading students in her classrooms, team members in corporate America, and now clients who hire her for coaching and team development services. She is grateful to use her teacher's heart and her businesswoman's mind to help those clients tap into their confidence and competence, both personally and professionally.

Tracy lives in her hometown of Staunton, Illinois with her husband, Jim. She has three children and five grandchildren who light up her world with soccer, baseball, wrestling, and imaginary food feasts.